Nothing Is Impossible shows you how to bring your full talents, including your hidden ones, to fruition. It provides an indispensable, highly valuable tool kit to radically improve your performance on a personal, social, and business level. This book is a must-read for anyone seeking to achieve major breakthroughs to inner peace and well-being and to fulfill their wildest dreams.

—Gary Fisher, Director, Objective Corporation Limited

The title *Nothing Is Impossible* reminds me of some sayings I have heard, such as "The sky's the limit!" I didn't know that there was a limit, actually. "You really think out of the box!" What box? I wonder. I like Tom Oliver's type of thinking, which he expresses so well in this book—it mirrors many of my own thoughts.

—Chip Davis, President and CEO, American Gramaphone Records, cofounder of Mannheim Steamroller

This book presents a tested and proven roadmap for anyone, entrepreneurs and professionals alike, to realize their true power, maximize their results, and make a unique contribution to society and the greater good at the same time.

—Salim Amin, Chairman, A24 Media/Camerapix

Tom Oliver found his groove as a musician, as a peacemaker, and now as an author. When you read *Nothing Is Impossible*, you will find your own groove as well, while discovering all those hidden talents you never thought you had.

—Chip Duncan, President of the Duncan Entertainment Group

Tom Oliver is the epitome of the social entrepreneur.

—James M. Brasher III, founding Director of the Global Philanthropists Circle

Nothing Is Impossible provides the right inspiration, tools, and easy-to-follow step-by-step instructions for how to attract the right partners and the best people to ensure the long-term success of any business or project. It also shows how to retain them.

—Ralph Buchholz, Senior Executive Recruiter,
Global Talent Acquisition, SAP

The determination and courage with which Tom organized The World Peace Festival in Berlin, where I was honored to speak, was Tom Oliver's way of showing that nothing is impossible.

—Gopi Kallayil, Chief Evangelist, Google Social for Brands

NOTHING
IS
IMPOSSIBLE

NOTHING
IS
IMPOSSIBLE

**7 Steps to REALIZE YOUR TRUE POWER
and MAXIMIZE YOUR RESULTS**

TOM OLIVER

New York   Chicago   San Francisco   Athens   London
Madrid   Mexico City   Milan   New Delhi
Singapore   Sydney   Toronto

1 2 3 4 5 6 7 8 9 0 DOC/DOC 1 9 8 7 6 5 4 3

ISBN   978-0-07-183122-2
MHID   0-07-183122-3

e-ISBN   978-0-07-183123-9
e-MHID   0-07-183123-1

Library of Congress Cataloging-in-Publication Data
Oliver, Tom.
 Nothing is impossible: 7 steps to realize your true power and maximize your results / Tom Oliver.
    pages cm
   ISBN 978-0-07-183122-2 (hardback) -- ISBN 0-07-183122-3 (hardback) 1. Success in business.
2. Management. 3. Goal (Psychology) 4. Success. I. Title.
   HF5386.O465 2014
   650.1--dc23   2013024266

McGraw-Hill Education books are available at special quantity discounts to use as premiums and sales promotions or for use in corporate training programs. To contact a representative, please visit the Contact Us pages at www.mhprofessional.com.

For *you*:

who are drawn to read this book,

to live a life beyond mediocrity and compromise to create the most fulfilled reality you can experience. This book is for you.

I dedicate this book:

To my father,

ERHART,

for his unwavering belief in me and his lifelong commitment, dedication, and loyalty.

To my mother,

MARGARETE,

for showing me the true value of speech and that a word can change worlds.

To my wife,

SIMONE,

for believing in me no matter what and for constantly teaching me the Brazilian way of ease and effortlessness.

To my English teacher at Choate,

CHUCK D. TIMLIN,

for showing me how to trust in myself as a writer and a speaker at a time when it mattered most.

SUPPORT WORLD EDUCATION—

Ten percent of all global author royalties from this book will be donated to the World Peace Foundation's "Rising Angels" project in partnership with the National Education Society of India (NES). Funds will go directly to the NES school in Dharavi, Mumbai, bringing education to impoverished and underprivileged kids in the largest slum in Asia: www.world-peace-foundation.org.

Contents

Foreword

My assistant came into my office. "There's a guy outside your office with shells around his neck and a crazy pair of Nikes. He says he has a meeting with you."

That's how I met Tom. Our business in Germany had been working with him on the creation of the World Peace Festival brand and Tom had asked if we could meet so that he could tell me all about the festival, the foundation, his mission, and how we could help.

"Don't forget you have a call in 30 minutes," my assistant said.

Two hours later Tom left my office. I had a new mission—to bring peace to the world—and a new friend.

During one of our early conversations, Tom and I talked extensively about the need for peace in the business world—not as some antidote or desire to escape the heat of competition, but as a necessary condition for success and a potential source of competitive advantage.

The notion of creating peace within an organization—reducing internal conflict, promoting harmony, and ultimately allowing for more collaboration and higher levels of innovation and creativity— makes eminent sense and offers obvious benefits. Tom helped me view a big business problem from a different perspective: I realized that breaking down silos within organizations could be tackled by seeking peace among the employees, and greater workplace harmony leads to more collaboration, less waste, and a more connected experience for customers.

Working at Interbrand, I have been lucky enough to meet and work with many of the world's business leaders, and it's clear that the themes explored in this book are, or should be, at the top of the agenda for any leading company.

As global competition intensifies and the digital world increases the speed of interaction between businesses and their customers, the need for creativity within businesses, flexible leadership styles, and the very best talent aren't just nice to have, they are a *must*-have if you want to stay ahead.

People the world over have high expectations from the companies they do business with and work for, and the biggest drivers of change over the next decade will be ever-more significant shifts in expectations—the expectations of increasingly digital consumers and the millennial generation—as well as a greater need for corporate citizenship.

These themes create a clear agenda for business leaders: Creativity and innovation will be vital to stay ahead of competition. Hiring and retaining the very best won't simply be a question of cash, it will be increasingly won by new leadership styles and corporate flexibility. And linked to both of these themes, corporate citizenship will increase its influence in attracting talent, customers, and investors.

Tom's natural creative flair and his ability to shift the way you think make him an excellent source of inspiration to anyone seeking to stay one step ahead. By drawing on his wide-ranging experiences and expertise as a global social entrepreneur, creative artist, businessman, singer and songwriter, live performer, speaker, philanthropist, and professor, Tom brings diverse themes for personal and professional success into his narrative, and these themes come to life in an exciting, inspirational, and motivational way.

On a final personal note, I love working with Tom. He instinctively brings a fresh viewpoint, and more importantly, he loves to collaborate and to explore. With his background in the world of music, it's hardly surprising that we both now regard our relationship as one long jam session. The beauty of jam sessions, of course, is that exciting and unexpected things always happen.

Jez Frampton, Global Group CEO, Interbrand

Preface: My Personal Story

I had just finished my first lecture at the Manchester Business School and was stepping out into the hallway when a student came up to me.

"Tom, can I ask you a question?" he said.

"Sure," I answered. "Shoot."

He asked: "What advice do you have for people to whom success hasn't come easily?"

I looked at him, puzzled, and replied: "But I never said it came easily for me."

And unfortunately, it didn't.

I wasn't born with a silver spoon in my mouth. And I wasn't born with a big name or a trust fund, either.

On the one hand, this book represents the collective wisdom of my personal work and interaction with the world's leaders and ultra-successful superperformers.

On the other hand, it also represents the essence of my personal challenges and how I solved them and turned them into my greatest assets and successes:

- From being a heavy stutterer who couldn't get a word out in class since age five to speaking five languages fluently and becoming a celebrated global keynote speaker who is invited by governments, heads of state from China to the United Nations, the world's premier financial institutions, such as the World Bank, political powerhouses like the European Parliament, elite organizations like the Young Presidents Organization, and cutting-edge corporations like Google in Silicon Valley.

- From being told by my kindergarten teacher and psychologists that I would be "unfit for school or higher education" to becoming an A student, receiving scholarships from the best boarding schools in the world, skipping grades, graduating with honors in several countries, getting into the best universities, and teaching global entrepreneurship at the best global business schools from Manchester to Kellogg School of Management.

- From being struck down as a teen by nervous tics, twitches, uncontrolled head jerking, shoulder shrugging, and involuntary body spasms that made me walk the streets like a zombie on acid to becoming a kung fu black belt who kitesurfs 20-foot waves around the world with his buddies from Maui.

- From being a skinny guy who always used to be the last one picked for any team to coaching some of the best surfers in the world on how to reach their peak performance.

- From being born into a family without means to becoming a recognized global social entrepreneur who was invited by the Rockefeller family to join the Global Philanthropists Circle, called "the most elite club in the world" by *BusinessWeek*.

- From having no contacts at all to founding one of the most respected peace organizations in the world, which has been praised by Nobel laureate Desmond Tutu as a "milestone for our times" and "the most influential peace gathering in history." (The World Peace Foundation and World Peace Festival have been supported by many dignitaries and Nobel laureates from around the world and by an impressive list of international partners, from the United Nations to Virgin Unite and Google, Hollywood actors and heads of state, global CEOs and entrepreneurs, world famous artists and leading philanthropists like Warren Buffett's son Peter.)

- From growing up in a sterile and creativity-free environment to becoming a world-renowned singer, songwriter, artist, pianist, and music producer whose iconic tracks are played by the most famous clubs from Tokyo to New York and who has been headlining music festivals around the world, from St. Tropez to Ibiza, as a live performer.

- From being bullied at school to becoming an "extraordinary leader" (Deepak Chopra) who has been praised by the world's leading agencies like Interbrand as a "gateway to millions of next generation trend setters and earlier adopters," whose "passion is contagious," and who has been awarded lifelong seats in the leading committees and think tanks of our time, from the Committee of 100 for Tibet to the Club of Budapest, along with a wide range of Nobel laureates and heads of state.
- From being born without a big name in a small town in Germany to creating one of the biggest and best first-class networks on the planet from scratch.
- From growing up in a rigid environment to becoming a globally recognized innovator who is called upon by cutting-edge corporations like Google to present whole new creative levels of solutions and who is described as "one of the most creative people on the planet" by the masterminds behind the award-winning viral Barack Obama "Yes, We Can!" campaign.

Because of my unique background, skill set, in-depth expertise, and experience as an artist, singer and songwriter, global entrepreneur, keynote speaker, professor, philanthropist, and leader, people have often called me a visionary and a modern Renaissance man.

If you live in so many worlds at once, you see things that others don't. This allows me to draw unsuspected parallels among all those different disciplines. It allows me to see the unifying principles that govern the outcomes of our actions.

It allows me to see and present the challenges and principles that govern our lives and the lives of the high achievers of this world in a new light.

This is the beauty and uniqueness of this book.

I will tell you to look bad, and then to look like a million dollars. I will tell you to care like crazy about the results you produce, then I will tell you that results don't matter, because language goes only so far, and it's all in the game.

I will show you that anyone can apply the best practices of creative artists to help him or her dramatically improve his or her life, career, or business.

I will try my best to shake up your world and take you on a roller-coaster ride, at the end of which you will come out having a lot more fun and being better at everything you do—no matter who you are and no matter where you are.

To overcome my personal challenges and turn them into my greatest successes, I have applied the same key principles as other high achievers.

If I can do it, you can do it. And I will show you how.

Do the impossible—because nothing is impossible.

Introduction

We are not in control of our lives: Principles are.
—Stephen Covey, *First Things First*

Are you ready to become the best you can be? Ready to dramatically improve your life, career, or business? Ready to leave a world of compromise and mediocrity behind to realize your true potential? Ready to grow into the person you've always wanted to become? Then this book is for you.

Most of us have been trained, educated, and brainwashed ever since we were born to settle for second best and go for Plan B. But I believe this is not who you really are.

If deep inside of you there's still that yearning desire to reach for the stars, discover your true power, and live the life of your dreams, then this book is for you.

FAQ: Is This Book for You?

Do I Need to Be Born Rich?

No. I wasn't born with a silver spoon in my mouth or a trust fund. Most of the billionaires I know were not born rich.

And most of the high achievers in my network, from Hollywood actors to world-famous artists, bestselling authors, world leaders,

Silicon Valley giants, leading philanthropists, Fortune 500 CEOs, and global entrepreneurs, were not born rich, either.

Contrary to popular belief, a lot of the sons and daughters of the well-known billionaire families have struggled with their wealth, their name, and their upbringing. It's hard to see that when you are on the other side. But trust me: not being born rich can be a great asset and motivator to help you realize your true potential and bring out the best in you.

Do I Need to Have a Top-Notch Education?

No. As you will see, a lot of the people who graduate from the Harvards of the world are also some of the most fearful. It took me years to get that Ivy League nonsense out of my head and create real success.

Most of the mind-blowing entrepreneurs who have created global empires, including self-made billionaires like Richard Branson and Bill Gates, didn't need a top-notch education to get where they are today. In fact, most of them chose to drop out of university or didn't even apply. They listened to their hearts, defined where they wanted to go, cut to the chase, and went straight for their goals. So can you. And I will show you how.

Do I Need to Be Born with a Big Name?

No. All you need to open any door you desire and create a first-class worldwide network from scratch is a vision, passion, and the courage to take action. Forget the big name.

Do I Need to Have a Lot of Time?

No. In fact, this book was designed for people with a busy lifestyle. What are the smallest necessary steps that will produce the biggest changes and dramatically improve your life, career, or business? Do you want to get results fast? Do the exercises. Most of the exercises in each chapter take only between 30 seconds and 5 minutes to complete and can be done anywhere, anytime. They are your power workout to get you into your best shape.

There's no need for fancy equipment. A paper and a pen, and you're in business! This ensures that you can put these exercises into practice immediately, wherever you are.

This book was born out of the need to teach people to get results fast. At the same time, it generates the momentum you need to create lasting change in your life, career, or business.

Do I Need to Have a Lot of Talent?

No, you don't. Talent is way overrated. In fact, some of the most talented people I know are miserable, broke, and hopelessly underachieving. Why? Because society has taught us that talent is everything. So what are they missing?

When it comes to creating success in all its forms, from wealth to happiness, from a fulfilled and balanced life to landing your dream job, from starting your own business to becoming the next Steve Jobs, vision, passion, and a clear sense of where you are going are much more important.

In fact, it's scary and refreshingly surprising what blatant weaknesses and talent-free zones most of the successful people who are at the top of their game have. It doesn't matter whether they are famous Hollywood actors, Grammy Award–winning artists, self-made entrepreneurs, or global CEOs. What they have understood and mastered, however, are a few key principles. This is what inspired me to write this book.

Do the impossible—because nothing is impossible!

How to Use This Book

This book contains a tested and proven seven-step plan.

Almost every section has an anecdote or personal story, a principle or lesson, one or more exercises, and a takeaway (Points to Remember).

The best way to use this book is to read it from start to finish. While I recommend that you read the material in the book in the order in which it was written, it was designed to fit your busy lifestyle. This is why each section can be read separately.

Want to skip ahead? Feel free. I'm a big believer in trusting your own energy. If you feel drawn to read a particular step or section first, go for it!

Want to get a quick review or brush up on what you've read before that next important meeting? Just look at the Points to Remember.

Why You Need This Book

In my role as founder and chair of the Leadership Circle at one of the best business schools in the world, the Manchester Business School, I've come in contact with many bright and talented students from more than 32 countries. I'm constantly impressed with their skills, motivation, drive, willingness to succeed, and dedication to making a difference.

Yet they consistently tell me of the tremendous struggles they face while trying to make sense out of their lives, to find their true passion, and to create real success—a success that includes not only their dream job, starting their own business, or taking their career to the next level, but also a healthy, balanced, and fulfilled life, a life well lived. They sense a gnawing lack of completion. They have a feeling that there is more out there, and that they could become and accomplish so much more if they were only given the right keys.

They have pressing questions like:

- How can I find time for what I really want to do?
- How can I find what I am truly passionate about?
- How can I achieve wild success doing what I love to do?
- How can I have fun and accomplish everything I ever dreamed of and more?
- How can I eliminate fear from my dictionary and live life unconditionally?
- How can I set goals that really work?
- How can I overcome self-doubt for good and skyrocket to success?

- How can I finally live the life of my dreams and dramatically improve my life, career, or business?

We have been told that if we deny ourselves our desires and passions, suppress our energy, sacrifice and compromise our unique individuality, and work a bit harder, we will get there one day.

I strongly disagree.

What happens? For most of the people I have met, the result is disillusion, frustration, burnout, and a loss of hope, sense, and accomplishment. In short, they end up with Plan B, C, or D instead of Plan A.

The fact that you picked up this book tells me that you can probably identify with them. For years, we have been given tools, methods, and techniques for creating success and managing our lives. Unfortunately, and this is where Richard Branson is right, the most important keys are not taught at business school or any other school or university.

To learn how to create real success, realize your true potential, and maximize your results, you have to look at the people who have done what you want to accomplish—the top achievers, the ultra-successful superperformers who push the boundaries of what the rest of the world thinks is possible. The people who truly believe that nothing is impossible.

What has surprised me the most in my personal interaction and work with world leaders, dignitaries like Desmond Tutu and the Dalai Lama, bestselling authors like Deepak Chopra and Paulo Coelho, pop icons like will.i.am, rock stars like Bono, leading philanthropists like the Rockefeller and Buffett families, self-made billionaires, global entrepreneurs, Fortune 500 CEOs, and business leaders like Richard Branson is that they all apply the same principles to succeed.

The book you are holding in your hands is a collection of these principles.

It represents the results and collective wisdom from hundreds of meetings with the world's top achievers from all areas, spanning more than a decade. These are the key principles that got them to where they are today.

It represents a dramatically different approach to personal and professional success and fulfillment. In one sense, it's very new. In another, it's very old, for these timeless principles govern our lives.

It's Tested. It's Proven. It Works.

In this book, these principles are laid out in a tested and proven seven-step plan. This plan is the basis for the success of not only high achievers like the ones just mentioned, but also countless other individuals who are at the top of their field or industry.

It represents the answer to one central question: how can we *all* realize our full potential and maximize our results—no matter who we are, and no matter where we are?

This plan will get you from good to great or from great to world-class in no time, wherever and whoever you are.

It has propelled countless global MBA students and clients of mine to new heights. It has given them not only more success than they ever thought possible, but also a sense of clarity, purpose, meaning, fulfillment, and balance.

Here are some of their comments:

"It helps you see whole new levels of solutions."

"The short duration of the exercises forces you to put them into practice immediately. You can see their momentum and effectiveness right away."

"It gives me the courage to follow my dreams and shows me how to make them reality."

"Personal stories and anecdotes make the principles come alive instead of just presenting the theory."

"Really useful, written in a simple and straightforward style."

"All the practical tips, tools, and best practices can be put to use immediately."

"The exercises are engineered to produce results now."

I will show you how to change your life, career, or business dramatically in as little as 30 seconds to 5 minutes a day.

You will learn:

- How to set goals that really work and accomplish everything you´ve ever dreamed of
- How to do what you love and end up with more time, money, focus, energy, and success in all areas of your life
- How creativity can help you unleash your true power
- How to get your best ideas
- How to turn every failure into victory
- How to quickly turbocharge your energy
- How to generate the best opportunities
- How to exude self-confidence and charisma wherever you go
- How to create a first-class worldwide network from scratch with no big name and no cash
- How to develop and sell a powerful personal or corporate vision
- How to put yourself into a state of peak performance where your best results happen with ease
- And much more

So read on—and enjoy the journey.

NOTHING
IS
IMPOSSIBLE

Step 1

Define Your Destination

Every Journey Needs a Destination— The Power of Your Personal Vision

Your time is limited, so don't waste it living someone else's life. . . .
Have the courage to follow your heart and intuition. They somehow
already know what you truly want to become. Everything else is secondary.
—Steve Jobs

Don't dream too small.
—Marc Allen, entrepreneur

Choose the Most Fulfilled Reality You Can Experience— Forget About Plan B!

This chapter is about developing your own personal vision—the vision of what your ideal life can (and will) look like if everything goes as perfectly as it possibly could.

It is about going for your ideal, for everything you want out of life. It was inspired by an exercise that was first introduced to me by my friend Marc Allen. He used it to lift himself out of poverty, create a multimillion-dollar publishing enterprise, and truly live the life of his dreams.

1

Like so many of us, I grew up in a culture that encourages people to go for Plan B and not for their ideal. This is based on the belief that you need to work on your safety net before you try reaching for the stars. I couldn't disagree more!

All the individuals I know who have achieved outstanding results in any area—from world-famous athletes, artists, actors, and philanthropists who have started worldwide movements to CEOs of billion-dollar corporations and self-made billionaires—have done so because they believed in their dreams, reached for the stars, and didn't let their lives slip away.

On the other hand, I also know countless individuals who are so focused on locking in Plan B that they forget all about Plan A—for their entire life!

I often start my speeches at schools, universities, and business schools with the opening sentence: "I want you to create the most fulfilled reality that you can experience!" The look on people's faces is priceless. I guess we're not used to going for Plan A anymore.

People on their deathbed will tell you that time flies. So you need to go for it *all*! Don't live someone else's dream.

The Power of a Personal Vision

Surround yourself with the right people, those who will tell you that it can be done, will give you the courage to pursue your dreams and your ideal life, and will support you as you do so.

Don't listen to the dream stealers—and there will be lots of them. Even people with the best of intentions will tell you that it can't be done. Those whose intentions are less honorable will tell you that it can't be done because they don't want you to succeed. Your success would put them to shame or remind them of how great they could be. Since most people are afraid of using their full power and energy, anything that reminds them of what they could actually be doing with their lives and what they could actually accomplish is scary. So they prefer that you lead a life of utter mediocrity, conforming to the status quo.

Believe in yourself, your vision, your dreams, your ideals, and your goals. Once you actually start to write down your personal vision of your ideal life, it will have already become a reality within your mind. Kids know how to do that far better than adults.

I love to work with kids, because they still know how to dream.

In India, I gave several speeches to bright, young, talented schoolkids from around the world as part of an educational World Peace Congress that was conducted for and by students and that my World Peace Foundation had helped bring to life. It was the first one of its kind. Over 8,000 students from over 10 countries participated.

Through my foundation, I set up the Rising Angels project that sends teachers into the largest slum in Asia, Dharavi in Mumbai, India, to give underprivileged and impoverished kids who might otherwise be forced to work in factories by their parents the chance to receive an education, the right educational tools to create a better life, and someday maybe even live the life of their dreams. Ten percent of all global author royalties of this book will be donated to this Rising Angels project in partnership with the National Education Society of India (NES). Funds will go directly to the NES school in Dharavi.

Kids dream and create their own worlds. We lose that far too easily as we grow up.

Reminding ourselves of the playfulness we had as children, and the imaginary worlds we created, will give us more power, imagination, and energy when it comes to putting our adult version of our ideal dream life on paper.

Kids dream and play; this is how they grow. In the same way, we can grow into our own dream worlds just as easily.

Never underestimate the power of your personal vision in transforming your own life and the lives of others.

Conforming Is the Kiss of Death for Success

You have to not listen to the nay sayers because there will be many and often they'll be much more qualified than you and cause you to sort of doubt yourself.
—James Cameron

Only dead fish swim with the flow of the river.
—Chinese proverb

Most people believe that you can't be happy—you can't do what you love and still be successful. Most people do not believe that you can be yourself and succeed brilliantly. So you have to go against the grain.

If you push your boundaries, you will push the world's boundaries. You will encourage each and every other living soul on this planet to do the same.

We're all connected; we're all *one*. So whatever you accomplish will become a blueprint for others to follow.

Prove the dream stealers, the can't doers, and the naysayers wrong.

Nothing is impossible!

EXERCISE: Define Your Personal Vision

Time needed: 2–20 minutes

This exercise will help you find your own inner child again who wants to dream and knows no boundaries.

For a moment, I want you to suspend all your doubts and fears and write down what your ideal life would look like five or ten years from now. If this time frame doesn't feel right, substitute whatever time frame feels best and you're most comfortable with. I tend to write down the most fulfilled reality I can imagine, without putting a specific time to it.

Let your imagination run wild. Go for it *all*. There are no "can't dos" or "should dos." You can truly accomplish anything you put your mind to.

This ideal vision will become your daily companion. I want you to review it at least once a day. If you're a reader (meaning that you process information better by reading it), read it after you get up in the morning or before you go to bed. If you're a listener (meaning that you process information better by listening to it), record it on your smartphone and play it back at those times.

Mornings after getting up and evenings before going to bed are the most powerful times and have the maximum impact.

The Girl from New York City

A student in my Manchester Business School Leadership Circle told me that she had difficulty knowing what she wanted out of life. I told her to start writing down her own personal vision of her ideal life, and in just a few minutes she had already filled two pages!

I said: "See, you have no problem at all knowing what you want."

She looked at me in surprise. Once she put her mind to it, she could write down exactly what her ideal life would look like. This simple exercise has worked wonders for people in many countries.

If you see any obstacles, wipe them away and just put your ideal vision on paper, bit by bit. Put down whatever comes to mind, and leave no area of your life out.

Of course, you can always add to your vision later, and if you want to extend the time beyond 20 minutes, feel free to do so. But 2 minutes is already enough to open the floodgates and get the creative juices of your imagination flowing.

This personal vision exercise has a tremendously powerful effect, even if you are already a rock star, a famous athlete, the CEO of a big corporation, a multimillionaire, or a self-made entrepreneur, or if you've just graduated from Harvard with honors. It is the ticket to your own personal paradise, and it is living proof that this paradise already exists. Writing it down will make it feel more real and tangible.

Tune in to the excitement you felt as a child, when you were continuously growing and discovering new worlds every day, when each day felt like an exhilarating adventure. This child is still inside of you and wants you to reclaim that sense of adventure, discovery, and creation.

Use the magic powers you have. You are the captain of your ship; guide it!

There's No Need to Show It to Anyone!

A word of caution: at first, it's better not to show your vision to anyone. One exception would be when you are comparing personal visions with somebody in a personal or professional area because you want to decide whether you share the same ultimate goals and visions. That's fine, but use your vision for this area and this purpose only.

My point is simply this: don't look for validation. Don't ask anyone for permission to become the person you want to be.

If you believe in your ideal vision, eventually others will, too. Dream and the world will dream with you!

EXERCISE: Visualize, Visualize, Visualize!

> Logic will get you from A to Z. Imagination will get you everywhere.
> —Albert Einstein

Time needed: 5 minutes

Imagination provides the answers to most of our problems and challenges. This is why, at least once a day, I want you to go wild and imagine that ideal scene, living your ideal life.

Imagine that you're right there. See what it feels, smells, and looks like to be living the life of your dreams.

There are many different ways to do this, and I just want to give you a few different options:

1. You can take 5 or 10 minutes and give yourself verbal suggestions that sum up where you want to be in a short, concise statement: "I am . . . ," "I have . . . ," and so on.
2. You can listen to music you love without giving yourself any specific suggestions. Music is a great way to boost your imagination, like a magic carpet ride. Then guide your imagination to visualize your ideal scene.
3. You can combine the two (my favorite), surfing the music and then giving yourself suggestions that reinforce the mental images you create.
4. You can give yourself several suggestions for 5 minutes at a time, with each suggestion involving one major area of your life that is part of your ideal scene (health and fitness, family and personal relationships, finances, your professional life, spirituality, and so on).

All of these techniques work.

Some days I just listen to music and let my imagination run wild. On other days, I will stick to suggestions and see which short and simple statements have the best effect on my subconscious mind and give me the most energy.

This is not rocket science, so don't try to make it complicated! Again, kids do this all the time. They don't overthink, and they dream naturally.

Option: Cover Your Back!

Paulo Coelho, the Brazilian writer and fellow member of the Club of Budapest, once said that we live in exciting times because the World Wide Web is the biggest library ever created, and it's always open.

If you feel you need more of a mental boost if you are to believe in the world you're setting out to create and the life you want to experience, search the world and the web for positive examples of people who have done what you want to do or have pushed the boundaries as individuals to achieve outstanding results.

Search for what people have done that everybody said they couldn't. This will be your own personal confidence booster as you go for your dreams, the big picture, and that ideal vision you have in your heart.

> See, this just goes to show that you can
> accomplish anything you put your mind to!
> —Brad Pitt

> If you're just looking to your friend, coworker, husband,
> or wife for validation, be careful. It can stop a lot of
> multimillion-dollar ideas in their tracks in the beginning.
> —Sara Blakely, founder of Spanx

Points to Remember

All the people who have achieved outstanding results in any area did so because they believed in their dreams and reached for the stars.

We're all connected; we're all *one*. So whatever you accomplish will become a blueprint for others to follow. Surround yourself with the right people, those who will tell you that it can be done, will give you the courage to pursue your dreams and your ideal life, and will support you as you do so.

If you believe in the personal vision of your ideal life, eventually others will, too.

Never underestimate the power of your personal vision in transforming your own life and the lives of others. Dream and the world will dream with you!

Learn from Creative Artists to Find Your True Passion

> Passion is energy. Feel the power that comes
> from focusing on what excites you.
> —Oprah Winfrey

The guy looked at me. I could see the desperation in his eyes. We were gathered with about 30 students at a reception after one of my talks at the Manchester Business School. He said, "Tom, how do I find out what I *really* want? How do I know what I'm truly passionate about?"

Let's rewind to another scene a few years earlier.

I was having dinner with the Brazilian author Paulo Coelho at the Cannes Film Festival. Paulo has sold more than 100 million books, including *The Alchemist*, one of the 20 bestselling books of all time. He leaned over and said, "Tom, we as artists are passionate by nature. We fall in love every day!"

Artists Are Passionate by Nature

It's easy for artists to be passionate—that's our job. We fall in love with life, again and again and again.

A photographer falls in love with the way the light of the warm Tuscan sun is creating shades on a basket as it shines through the lattice windows in the old barn.

A musician falls in love with the sound of a rainstick as he is standing in the middle of a store in Paris. Swinging it from ear to ear and closing his eyes, he is fully immersed in the sound, as if warm summer rain were falling on his skin. People stop and stare, wondering what could be so exciting about a rainstick. To him, it's paradise!

A painter falls in love with the magical light in the South of France. It's calling him to take the canvas down into the garden and put heavy acrylic paint on it.

Writers fall in love with writing instruments, from simple pens to Montblanc masterpieces. I can't get enough of the sound of a ballpoint pen as words begin to form on paper with ease.

I recall that when I was a child, I longed for the moment when I would go to my father's office on the weekends and sit in front of the typewriter. When my fingers pressed down on the keys to create words, poems, and stories, it would send chills down my spine. It was a magical act!

Don't Use Your Intellect as a Stop Sign

It's amazing that the most important questions and answers are never taught in school. Instead, we are distracted, as by a magic trick, from the things that matter most. We waste many years of our lives chasing somebody else's dream or barking up the wrong tree.

Perhaps the biggest question of all is the one the guy at Manchester Business School asked me: "What is it that I really want? What am I truly passionate about?"

We have been taught, schooled, and trained not to go for what we want, but we admire the people who do! In fact, 99.9 percent of all the people I've ever met seem to have a problem with this.

People from all walks of life ask me again and again where I get my seemingly never-ending energy from. The answer is simple: I'm obsessively passionate about life. This has a great upside: it makes it easier for me to help those who have a hard time figuring out what it is that excites them the most.

Let Your Spontaneity Guide You

We have been conditioned to believe that we cannot trust our own intuition, our most natural leanings, or the things that we gravitate toward most easily. This is based on a deep distrust of ourselves and our nature.

But we are born with the opposite: a deep natural trust in ourselves and the life and energy that is within us. Kids naturally gravitate toward what they love most. In the end, it's the easiest thing to do. Our most natural inclinations point the way for us.

As adults, we are afraid of what we might find if we ask the most important question of all. What might happen once we realize how much time we've wasted chasing the wrong dream? We are too afraid that we won't be able to reach our goals. As Paulo puts it, there are two main reasons why people don't reach their goals and accomplish their wildest dreams: distraction and a fear of failure.

One of the most important assets and tools that we have available when it comes to finding our own answers and our deepest passions is our spontaneity.

Unfortunately, this is also one of the most underrated, misunderstood, and distrusted elements in our society. We live in a world of collective ignorance that is only slowly waking up to a new level of consciousness. This is why we fear that spontaneity will create more problems than it solves. We distrust it. We think it leads to chaos. We use our intellect as a stop sign rather than letting it shout, "Go!" when we are being truly spontaneous.

But it is exactly that spontaneity that leads us to our own answers, to our own inner and deepest knowing, and to our life's passion.

Our inner being speaks through our spontaneity. It automatically points to the solution of our problems and our challenges and to our greatest passions.

So, in essence, the answer lies in simplicity itself.

Spontaneity automatically leads to the most fulfilled reality we can experience. It promotes wealth, health, and happiness, and it leads to a natural order in our life, not chaos. This includes putting our passion first.

EXERCISE: Find Your True Passion

Step 1: Rediscover the Child Within
Time needed: 5 minutes

The goal is to list the five things that you were most passionate about as a child.

To get you going, start with the very first thing that comes to mind.

Then take it a step further. Think about other things and activities that excited you most when you were young.

If you are not immediately successful at this, don't give up. Set aside another time and go at it again for five minutes. Be patient. Sometimes many layers have to be peeled away before you can get to the obvious, especially if you've spent years burying your dreams and passions deep down inside you. You will find that the second time will already be a lot easier because your subconscious will have begun to work on the answers.

Step 2: Take It to Puberty
Time needed: 5 minutes

Now skip to puberty and your teenage years. If you are honest with yourself, most of your natural inclinations, spontaneous leanings, and greatest passions will again surge visibly and clearly during this period.

It doesn't matter whether you acted on them or not. For now, remembering them will suffice.

After you have again listed five activities or things that you were most passionate about during this period of your life, look at the two lists, compare them, and see what obvious parallels there are.

Then marry them. Decide which are the five activities that you will try over the next five weeks.

Five Weeks to Your New Life—A Life Filled with Passion and Purpose
Again, start small. Choose one of those five activities and schedule it in your diary as a "passion field trip" for the upcoming week.

Don't chicken out! We will get you back to what you love, but you have to be patient and stick with it.

Then, the following week, take another activity from your list and schedule it.

There is no reason to assign priorities to these activities or to put them into a particular order. Just doing them one by one will be enough.

After these five weeks, take a good look at yourself. Which activity excited you most? Which one filled you with a strong sense of discovery and purpose?

Regardless of the immediate outcome, over time, this simple exercise will bring you closer to discovering your true passion and what you love most. It may take a while, but you've set wheels in motion that are unstoppable.

Those five weeks will have astounding effects. Like small ripples in an ocean, they will soon produce giant waves that will take you to your paradise island.

It won't be long before you are sailing through life with a newfound energy that you never thought possible—an energy that will be unlimited because you will feel the winds of passion blowing in your sails!

If passion drives you, let reason hold the reins.
—Benjamin Franklin

Only in spontaneity can we be who we truly are.
—John McLaughlin, guitarist

Points to Remember

To find out what you really want and what you are truly passionate about, you first have to learn to trust your spontaneity.

It is our spontaneity that leads us to our own answers, to our own inner and deepest knowing, and to our life's passion. Our inner being speaks through our spontaneity. It automatically points to the solution of our problems and our challenges. Spontaneity leads to the most fulfilled reality we can experience. It promotes wealth, health, and happiness, and it leads to a natural order in our life, not chaos. This includes putting our passion first!

The things and activities you were most passionate about as a child and as a teenager can give you important clues when it comes to finding what matters most to you. A life filled with purpose and a never-ending reservoir of energy await!

How to Find Your Ideal in All Areas of Your Life

I have the simplest tastes. I am always satisfied with the best.
—Oscar Wilde

All successful men and women are big dreamers. They imagine what
their future could be, ideal in every aspect, and then they
work every day toward their distant vision, that goal or purpose.
—Brian Tracy

The Manchester Business School was hosting a reception for me after my first lecture, and I was with a group of students from more than 32 countries. While we were sipping wine and enjoying the snacks, a half circle gathered around me. One of the students from the United States said, "Tom, I never know what I really want. I just went to my university career counselor and asked her for help, but it seems I just get more and more confused."

Let's put you back in the driver's seat and take you to Happiness Front Row. Here are some tools to help you discover what you really want—in all areas of your life—and get you closer to your ideal.

Tool 1: Your Personal Vision

I talk about defining your personal vision at length in a separate section.

To put it in a few words, you need a clear destination. You need to write down what your ideal life would look like 5 or 10 years from now. Think of your ideal, the end goal, and don't dream too small.

Leave nothing out. Go for it *all*!

Look for the *big* dream—the one that excites you, the one you are passionate about.

I started my first lecture at Manchester Business School with the following sentence: "I want you to go for the most fulfilled reality that you can experience!" The students looked at me with a mixture of bewilderment and excitement—he can't be serious!

I'm dead serious.

Go for *it all*!

Look at the big picture. Go for the Big Hairy Audacious Goals and take them even a bit further. Stretch yourself, your imagination, and the boundaries of what you think is possible. You will feel an energy pulling you out of bed every morning as if you were hanging on a magic string operated by a giant puppeteer. Your inner fire and love for life will soar.

Remind yourself that you can grow into that future as easily as you grew from the past into the present. That's a powerful image that I first read about in one of Jane Roberts's books. I myself have used that phrase often whenever I catch myself thinking: "It's hard. It can't be that easy. I can't get what I want."

You can. Go for your *ideal*!

Tool 2: Visualization

I will refer to this more when I discuss the "Hour of Power." For now, use visualization to find out what resonates most with you. Set aside time every day to visualize your ideal. Try out different scenarios, as if you were trying on different costumes for a stage performance.

Why do children love to dress up and try out different personas? Why are Halloween parties so much fun? Because we love to playfully slip into new characters. We try them on for size.

In a similar fashion, use your imagination to find the ideal future version of the life that you want to live—the one that excites you most; the one that liberates your energies; the one that makes you get out of bed every morning.

Use Music as a Rocket Booster to Reach the Life of Your Dreams

When you are visualizing the life of your dreams, try to use music that you love. It's a powerful tool because it stimulates visualization, makes mental images more vivid and colorful, and gives emotions more depth.

I have the most vivid imagery when I close my eyes and listen to music that I love. There is something magical about music that transcends all boundaries.

When you listen to music that you love, it takes you on a magic carpet ride to the most wonderful places in your mind. It will help you to discover what's ideal for you and what it is that you really want.

I even make a special playlist in iTunes with the songs that trigger the most vivid images in my mind at any given time.

Tool 3: The Visual Anchor

There are a lot of things I recommend in this book that are all geared toward making you focus on your ideal, on your desires and goals, on where you want to go. The vision board, the Hour of Power, the espresso experience, and the visualization exercises are just a few examples.

Now I want to introduce you to something simple that I use to help me keep my ideal focus.

It's an anchor, and it came to me during meditation.

When I get up in the morning, I write the number 1 in the palm of my left hand. It serves as a reminder that I should always focus on my ideal—the 1, as I call it—in every area of my life. I call it the 1 because it forces me to come up with one clear, conceptualized image of every one of my desires and goals, and to concentrate on them.

I apply this anchor of the 1 to any area, large or small, not just my big goals. If I have a meeting, it reminds me to focus on the ideal outcome of that meeting. Often we are so busy hurrying from one meeting, phone call, or task to the next that we don't even ask ourselves what the ideal outcome would be. No wonder we end up with mediocre results.

If I can't walk into a meeting with a small 1 written on the palm of my hand, I try something else as an anchor, ideally something that is placed in such a way that I need to look at it often.

Often, we don't even define what an ideal outcome would be. Or, if we do, we get distracted. A visual anchor will counter this by bringing a powerful focus into your life.

Tool 4: The Visual Trigger and the Most Important Question of All

Then use a visual trigger to ask yourself the question "Is this what I really want?" at various times throughout the day. This will help you focus on the mental images and activities that are in line with your ideal personal vision and your big-picture goals.

This idea came to me in a dream, and it has helped me greatly. I use my wedding ring to serve as a visual trigger because I see it often.

The question "Is this what I really want?" refers to whatever I'm doing (physically) or thinking about at the moment. This means that it tackles both the inside *and* the outside: "What mental images am I focusing on at the moment? Are these the images of the events and circumstances that I want to create and attract?" and "Am I doing what I really want to be doing at the moment?"

Steve Jobs put it in wonderful terms: "For the past 33 years, I have looked in the mirror every morning and asked myself: If today were the last day of my life, would I want to do what I am about to do today? And whenever the answer has been 'No' too many days in a row, I know I need to change something." His visual trigger was his bathroom mirror, and it served him well.

Use the visual trigger that works best for you. Ideally, it should be something that you see often, like a ring, bracelet, or watch, so that it reminds you to ask the question frequently enough to get you back on course.

Break Free from the Limiting Beliefs That Hold You Back

Let's handle the several blocks that can come up.

Limiting Belief 1: You Are Too Focused on the Details, the Specifics, Instead of on Your Goal

Artists are big dreamers. Be inspired by them and dream big. Dream of your ideal. Don't let the specifics get in the way.

Let me give you an example: your goal is to have a fulfilling, happy relationship with someone you love.

Now, that's a great goal! Let's say you meet somebody and think: "This has to be the one and no one else!" But at the same time, you might be ignoring impulses and intuitions that tell you otherwise.

If you fall into this trap, you are too fixated on the specifics rather than the end goal. You are saying: "Well, I want a happy relationship, but I think I can have it only with this one particular person."

And that's nonsense. Your soul mate might be right around the corner, and you could miss this great opportunity because you are so fixated on the specifics rather than the end goal.

Again, use Tool 4, the visual trigger, to get into the habit of asking yourself what you really want. This will prevent you from getting lost in the specifics that don't really matter.

The Student Without the Scholarship

Here's another example of an e-mail that I received:

> "I visualized a seat at business school with a scholarship, but I ended up with a seat without a scholarship. This does not mean that I ended up unhappy because of it, but the scholarship would have made my financial position so much better.
>
> I am not sure why, but it never happened the exact way I visualized it."

A better visualization would have been to see himself graduate successfully, which is the end goal he really wanted to accomplish.

Let's imagine for a moment that the end goal he was really after was to start his own business after graduation. Life could have given him a shortcut, but it was too early for him to see it. Not having a scholarship might have led him to look for a part-time job to finance his studies. At his new job, he might just have met the right person to start his own business with, and ended up a happy self-made entrepreneur! The Rolling Stones met while they were students at the London School of Economics and then went on to become one of the most successful rock bands of the twentieth century.

In the film *The Best Exotic Marigold Hotel* one of the actors talks about an Indian saying that goes like this: "Everything will be all right in the end . . . if it's not all right then it's not yet the end."

If you focus on the end goal, your inner self and your life will work out the best way to take you there, but you have to trust the process. As Steve Jobs said: "You can't connect the dots looking forward."

Limiting Belief 2: You Ask Everybody but Yourself

Let's go back to the example of the business school student from New York City. She said, "Tom, I never know what I really want. I just went to my university career counselor and asked her for help, but it seems I just get more and more confused."

When I had her do the ideal scene for two minutes in class, she was able to put half a page of her ideal future on paper, across many different areas from her ideal relationship and her ideal working environment to her ideal social and family life. It was all there! And that in just two minutes. She knew exactly what she wanted when she was put to the test, so why all this confusion?

Her problem was that she had been running around like crazy asking everybody but herself what she really wanted. And, of course, she got a hundred different answers!

Once she used the ideal scene as an exercise to finally ask herself for advice, a magic door to a universe of countless answers opened.

Two minutes of her time spent looking inward was all it took. Learn from her example and don't ask others—ask yourself! You are your own ultimate and greatest authority.

Limiting Belief 3: You Don't Have the Right to Go for Your Dreams!

At the same reception at Manchester Business School, a timid guy who was dressed very conservatively asked me in a shy voice, "Tom, can I really go for my dreams, for what I really want? Do I have the right to go for my dreams? I have a family; I'm in debt. I have no choice . . . I can't go for my dreams."

Repeat after me: "Everybody has the right to go for her dreams." Everybody—including yourself.

I want you to take a pen and a sheet of paper and write: "I have the right to go for my dreams."

James Cameron, the famous director, dreamed the story of *Terminator* when he was 30 years old and broke. He acted on his vision. The rest is history. Many years later, the movie *Terminator* became his breakthrough, and in 2012 his net worth was estimated at $700 million. His career also includes being the director of the highest-grossing film of all time, *Avatar*.

All the self-made billionaires I know have one thing in common: they all got there because they were pursuing their dreams and didn't ask anyone else for permission.

Limiting Belief 4: You Might Be Taking Away from Others If You Go for What You Want

Well, my guess is just the opposite: you will make your biggest contribution.

I want you to write something else down: "Only by honoring myself do I truly honor others."

That's the "as you love yourself" part of the famous "Love your neighbor as you love yourself" commandment of Christian doctrine. We have stressed the "Love your neighbor" part far too much and forgotten about ourselves in the process! Our whole society and our educational system are built on self-denial and the belief that you can't do what you want.

The discussion of abundance in a later chapter will also help you a lot if you believe you might be taking away from others. The world is not a zero-sum game; abundance is the natural state of our being.

Limiting Belief 5: You Think in Terms of Either/Or, Not Both

A fellow in one of my Leadership Circle lectures at Manchester Business School asked me: "Tom, isn't it a contradiction to set a goal for myself in business and pursue that aggressively and set a goal for my spiritual development at the same time?"

In one of my seminars, a businesswoman from China asked a similar question: "Can I become a successful businesswoman and have a happy family life as well?"

Two very obvious limiting beliefs show in these questions: "You can't have what you want!" and "You can't have your cake and eat it, too."

Well, guess what? In most cases you can!

Things that may seem to be mutually exclusive at first are in reality two elements that are not in conflict. You can have both, but you have to start telling yourself that; if you don't, you will not see the solution.

The trick is to use suggestions to tell yourself, "I can have both" instead of being stuck in an "either . . . or" decision. You *can* have both.

All the great high achievers, fulfilled self-made entrepreneurs, CEOs, and top performers do exactly that.

Once you realize that you can have both, life will open up countless doors and bring you the right opportunities to show you that, indeed, you can. The belief that you can't is itself the problem. Once you change it, you will start to create and attract ideas, solutions, and circumstances that allow you to have both.

EXERCISE: Write Down Your Personal Vision

Time needed: 2 minutes

Schedule 30 minutes in the course of the next seven days to read the section on the power of your personal vision and actually sit down and develop it—if you haven't already done so.

EXERCISE: Decide on a Visual Anchor

Time needed: 30 seconds

Decide right now what would be a good visual anchor to remind you to focus on the ideal in all areas of your life. It doesn't have to be perfect—any visual anchor will do, as long as you see it often.

Use your visual anchor to ask yourself again and again: "Is that what I really want?"

EXERCISE: Choose a Visual Trigger

Time needed: 30 seconds

Let's face it: as kids we knew exactly what we wanted, even with the smallest things. It's that Popsicle, not this one. It's the red sweater, not the blue one. We didn't care what others thought; we just went with our own natural impulses.

We have to relearn this behavior that was so natural for us long before we were educated and learned to "grow up." We have to get in touch with our inner child, the one who always knew what we wanted.

That child in you has grown, but it still knows. Let's give it some room.

The trick, again, is to start small. Use a visual trigger that works for you and that you see frequently enough to get you back on course. Use it to ask yourself in simple, everyday situations: "What is it that I really want right now?" Start with your lunch or dinner choice tonight or your choice of clothes tomorrow morning. The little things will get you to the biggies.

That's it! You have just taken the first steps toward getting closer to the life of your dreams!

Points to Remember

Use your personal vision as the tool to decide what you really want and as a guide to create the most fulfilled reality you can experience.

Set aside time every day to visualize your ideal. Use music as a powerful tool to stimulate your visualization, make your mental images more vivid and colorful, and give your emotions more depth.

Use a visual anchor to remind yourself to always focus on the ideal outcome of your goals, plans, and projects—not the problems, obstacles, or challenges. This visual anchor will also be a powerful reminder and focus to help you define what the ideal outcome would be in each and every area of your life.

Use a visual trigger to ask yourself the question: "Is this what I really want?" at various times throughout the day. This will help you focus on the mental images and activities that are in line with your ideal personal vision and your big-picture goals.

Break free from the limiting beliefs that hold you back:

1. Dream of your ideal, but don't let the specifics get in the way.
2. Don't ask others—ask yourself! You are your own ultimate and greatest authority.
3. Keep telling yourself that you have the right to go for your dreams.
4. Realize that you are not taking away from others if you set out to create the most fulfilled reality you can experience. The contrary is true: only by honoring yourself do you truly honor others.
5. Think in terms of "both," not "either/or." Once you realize that you can have both, life will open up countless doors and bring you the right opportunities to show you that, indeed, you can. The belief that you can't is itself the problem. Once you change it, you will start to create and attract ideas, solutions, and circumstances that allow you to have both.

Set Goals That Really Work and Accomplish Everything You've Ever Dreamed Of

And, you know, it's a blessing because I know what I want
and I have goals, and I've met so many of my goals. And I just keep
making new goals, because I'm never satisfied and I always want to grow.
—Beyoncé Knowles

Everything changes.
—The Buddha

I get this question a lot: "Why do the goals that I set for myself not work?" Or, in simpler terms: "Why do I not reach my goals?"

Today we have hundreds of books with endless good advice about goal setting, and a lot of them tell you to do different things. No wonder people get confused and become so frustrated that they literally give up on setting goals and put their life on autopilot.

Here's my guide to proper personal goal setting.

If your goals are to work, three things are essential:

1. You have to embrace change and yourself on a deeper level. This means embracing what you really want: your wishes, desires, and dreams.
2. Your goals need to have your internal buy-in. This is what I call the inner agenda of goal setting.
3. You need to constantly impress your goals on your subconscious mind.

Let's tackle these things one by one.

Embrace Change

I was just about to put my pullovers in the closet downstairs, and I thought, "I really want to move to another country, to a warmer climate. I hate it here. And I would love to do this by the end of next year." But then I immediately started to second-guess myself: "Do I have the right to go for what I really want? Is that wish justified?"

Then I heard a voice say: "Embrace change; embrace yourself—what you want and your wishes."

I was in a dream. After I woke up, I wrote everything down. A few months later, way before my deadline, I moved into my new ocean view home in the South of France—with the sun and a smile on my face.

When we talk about goal setting, we talk about an inner mindset that you have to cultivate. One of the biggest issues is "change." A lot of people resist change. We all do to some degree.

The people who really get things done and accomplish their dreams embrace change. They see change as a chance to bring more of what they want into their lives—a chance to fulfill their dreams.

And if they listen closely, they can even hear the grass of change growing: the little indications that they are on the right track, that their intentions are beginning to materialize. You might call them the first little drops of the summer rain or, as Paulo Coelho put it to me, the signs that you are on the right path.

Change is life; life is change. Get over it. Embrace it!

Change is your chance to reach your goals, to live the life you have always dreamed of, and to experience the most fulfilled reality you can imagine.

Embrace Yourself: Your Desires, Goals, and Dreams

The second part of the sentence I heard was, "embrace yourself."

This whole book is about encouraging you to follow your dreams, so it's way too much to cover in one chapter. If you read the rest of the book, you'll be fine.

Throughout the book, I encourage you to be the person you really want to become—to grow into that *bigger you*, a phrase that I use often.

Giving up on setting goals means giving up on life.

Without desire, there's no life. As the author Jane Roberts wrote in her bestselling Seth books series: "Desires are as natural as a cat's whiskers. As desire is born, so shall being be born."

Desire is the most natural part of life and of your being. To embrace yourself means to embrace your desires, goals, and dreams.

Your Internal Buy-In—the Inner Agenda of Goal Setting

Your goals have to come from inside you and have to have your *inner approval* if they are to work properly. That's why so many people fail at goal setting: there's no inner buy-in. Then they conclude that goal setting just doesn't work for them. It does, but their failure means that they set their goals on a superficial level.

We all have an inner agenda that we have to take into consideration when we're setting our goals.

Let's go back to my dream. My goal was spontaneous. It was true desire, born out of the joy of my being, spontaneously, in the moment. This is why it worked so well when I put it into practice: because my whole being was behind it.

You have to go with that inner force of your being.

If you are unsure whether a goal is right for you, and it is, then either the impulse to set the goal will come up again and again over time or it will be so strong that you just know it's right. It's a lot like being in love—when you are, you just know it. It clicks.

The love comparison is a good one. Trust your own inner spontaneous guidance system and intuition in setting your goals. It knows what's best for you.

Constant Impression and the 1,000 Helping Hands

Constant impression means that the goals you set for yourself have to be imprinted on your subconscious solidly enough that your mind, your subconscious, and the whole universe can set the mechanisms in motion that will bring you what you desire.

I call this the "1,000 helping hands."

Enough means "with the right frequency and intensity."

This is different for each person, and you have to work out and feel out what's best for you. Again, trust your own inner guidance system.

This also has a lot to do with how many goals you set for yourself. Lou Holtz, the famous American college football coach who is also the only one in NCAA history to lead six different programs to bowl games, set 101 goals for himself that he wanted to accomplish before he died.

The best impression is your own rhythm, which you have to find for yourself. This simply means how often you need to review your goals, either verbally, mentally, or visually, or by writing them down again and again.

There is no rule for this. An Asian billionaire writes down his goals every morning. Others just look at their vision board when they get up in the morning. Rockefeller was rumored to write his most important goals on an index card and review them every 15 minutes.

Should you set goals for days, weeks, and months as well? Do what works for you. Try it out. Again, there are no fixed systems, just endless examples.

You need just enough structure to keep you focused without being overwhelmed by too many goals.

For me right now, setting seven major goals, one for each of the seven major areas of my life, works just fine.

The Power of Crisis and a Major Breakthrough Goal

Deadlines have the magic of reducing everything to the essential.

Then there are crises, emergencies that put you into a powerful "one goal" mode—you know immediately what to focus on and what to do. That's the power of having one major goal.

Jack Canfield, the coauthor of the *Chicken Soup for the Soul* book series, which has sold more than 100 million copies around the world, set one major breakthrough goal: to produce his first *New York Times* bestseller.

There is a great advantage in setting a major breakthrough goal because it allows you to concentrate your "champion's attitude" (see Chapter 3) and its associated triggers and anchors on one single major goal, and thus you can reach it a lot faster.

By When?

This is really up to you as well. There is objectivity (expert's opinions, people who have done it before, and so on), and there is *you*. You may just push the boundaries of what's possible and do what no one has ever done before. All great inventors are terrific examples, from Tesla to Henry Ford and his Model T. Bill Gates at Microsoft gave his employees a deadline for when the new version of Windows should come out, and even though they had no idea how they would meet the deadline, they did. Bill saw that it was possible when no one else did.

When you are charting new territory, there's no precedent, there's just *you*. You have to believe in yourself and your own inner vision. That's why I keep telling you to include all of your senses, to live life to the fullest, and to keep your balance in all the major areas of your life. This will allow you to tap into your own inner guidance system much more effectively and come up with the goals that work for *you*!

EXERCISE: Set One Major Goal for Yourself

Time needed: 2 minutes

Take one goal for one major area of your life. Put down what the goal is and by when you want to achieve it. Then play with three different versions of the same goal, varying the "what" and the "by when."

Put those three different versions on index cards or little Post-its.

Carry them in your wallet.

Listen to your inner voice as you go about your business. Tune in to your intuitions and your spontaneous impulses.

Maybe you will feel the need to go over the cards again. That's fine.

Then, after three days, readdress the different versions and see which one sticks. Which version of the goal resonates with you most? Your subconscious will have begun to work on the different versions, and you will get inner feedback as to which one is right for you.

If none of them resonates with you, repeat the exercise until you have one goal that sticks and you "fall in love."

Then you can freely transfer your success in this goal-setting exercise to other areas of your life and set other goals.

Video Links

In YouTube, type "The Best Motivation Video." Be prepared for some surprises!

This is one of the best inspirational videos I have ever come across. It shows that you should stick to setting goals and shoot for the stars even if no one else believes in you.

It's also a great motivator if you ever come across some of life's big challenges—those times when everything sucks and even your friends throw you a curveball. We've all been there.

Points to Remember

For your goals to work, a few keys are essential:

1. You have to embrace change. Change is your chance to reach your goals, to live the life you have always dreamed of, and to experience the most fulfilled reality you can imagine.

2. You have to embrace yourself on a deeper level. This means embracing what you really want: your wishes, desires, and dreams.
3. We all have an inner agenda that we have to take into consideration when setting our goals. Your goals need to have your internal buy-in. Your spontaneity will give you important clues: goals that come up spontaneously again and again over time are usually the ones that work and stick.
4. Constantly impress your goals on your subconscious mind. This means that the goals you set for yourself have to be imprinted on your subconscious enough so that your mind, your subconscious, and the whole universe can set the mechanisms in motion that will bring you what you desire.

Look Where You Want to Go

Obstacles are the frightful things you see
when you take your eyes off your goal.
—Henry Ford, American industrialist

I was gliding down the Swiss Alps. Well, actually, I was sitting on my butt most of the time. I had just switched from skiing to snowboarding, and unfortunately, my body and the board were going in different directions.

I had a friend with me who had just placed first in the Swiss snowboard championships. "Tom," he said, "just look where you want to go, and your body and the board will follow."

I looked at the steep slope below me. It wasn't encouraging. I slowly turned the tip of my board into the fall line. The board started to accelerate and take on a life of its own, and I was scared.

"OK," I said to myself, "let's just try it. My butt can't hurt much more than it does now."

I turned my head in the direction I wanted to go and kept fixing my eyes on that point. Then the magic happened: my shoulders started to turn, the board turned as well, and I was gliding to my destination in pure bliss.

Since that moment, the simplicity of this rule has never ceased to amaze me. It's so simple that I have to constantly remind myself of it because it applies not only to sports, but to everything in life: "Look where you want to go, and the rest will follow."

Life will take care of the million changes necessary to take you toward your goal, just as it took care of the changes in body stance and movements of the snowboard when I was gliding down the Alps. But you have to look where you want to go.

You Can't Look at Obstacles

I love stand-up paddling. Now it has become as popular as my buddy Mike Eskimo, a famous waterman from Maui, predicted 10 years ago.

It was summer in the South of France. I was paddling past a group of hapless tourists who kept falling into the choppy water; it was their first time on their boards.

I explained: "Guys, you have to look at the horizon, not down at the board, not even a few feet away. Resist the urge to look at the waves that are coming in or whatever obstacle is a few feet away. Just keep your eyes fixed on the horizon, where you want to go, and this will take care of your balance automatically."

A few minutes later, the guys were paddling upright like Kelly Slater on coke, eyes steadily gazing into the distance . . .

When you are learning to kitesurf, the biggest challenge is learning to ride upwind, since the kite is actually pulling you downwind. On top of it all, you have to coordinate your body, the board, and the kite at the same time, which can be totally confusing. Again, the same magic principle applies: look where you want to go, keep your eyes fixed on your destination, don't look at the kite or the board, and go for it.

Then the rest of your body makes all the necessary adjustments magically—your shoulders follow the turn of your head; your knees change their angle; your feet change their stance. The board slowly turns in the right direction, and the kite places itself at the right spot. Off you go!

Everything Will Conspire to Take You to Your Goal

Many years later, I taught the philosophy of snowboarding to my friend Phillip, who was just starting out.

"The biggest challenge is to overcome your fear as you are pointing your board right down the fall line of the slope, and you gain speed. You have to surrender yourself to the mountain and the board in those initial moments, with full confidence and faith that you will be all right. Once you have gained speed, you look where you want to go, and that initiates the turn. Your body and the board will take care of it automatically. You don't have to worry about it. As soon as you interfere, you upset your balance, and you'll fall. You have to trust the board. You have to trust that the board will take you there if you continue to look where you want to go." This applies to any other area of life as well.

Just as your body makes miraculous adjustments and transfers these to the board as soon as you look where you want to go, your circumstances will just as surely change and make the necessary adjustments to take you toward your goal in all other areas of your life. But you have to trust the process.

The "1,000 helping hands" will come into play. Doors will open that you didn't even know existed; help will appear out of nowhere, aiding you in your journey towards your destination.

Riding Jaws, or How You Can Accomplish Extraordinary Things by Extraordinary Focus

Jaws in Maui is the biggest wave in the world, reaching heights of up to 65 feet or more.

My friend Mickey Eskimo showed me a picture of him riding that monster. It became an ad for a famous sports brand. He is six feet tall, but he looks tiny compared to that giant mass of water.

I was dying to get a question out. "Mickey," I asked, "what was it like to surf that wave? What went through your mind?"

His answer was disappointing to me at first, but it made all the more sense once I connected the dots.

"Tom, when I was riding down that wave, I didn't see the giant monster you are looking at now in the picture. I was so focused on the next step, the very next thing I had to do to get this done. I kept my eyes fixed on where I was going and was totally present in the moment. It actually wasn't that big of a deal when I was in it. Only looking at this picture later made me realize what I had really accomplished."

Simple Can Be Harder than Complex, Especially Today

In today's world, we are constantly bombarded by information over-kill, and we are trying to filter it all.

The more gifted you are intellectually, the more you may tend to complicate things and lose sight of simplicity, or looking where you want to go. We lose ourselves in details, in the little chops of the waves, in the minutiae, instead of riding the waves of our life with a smile.

We all aspire to something greater. What gets us through the hours of practicing until we reach mastery? Dedication, passion, knowing we will succeed?

Yes. But most of all, we need a clear focus on our destination. In the end, that's all that matters.

EXERCISE: The Magic Anchor

Time needed: 1 minute

As I stated earlier, you should use a visual anchor to remind yourself to always focus on the ideal outcome of your goals, plans, and projects—not the problems, obstacles, or challenges.

I often write the number 1 in the palm of my left hand to remind me of the conceptualized images of my desires. I call these "the 1s" because they stand for the one and only ideal goal or outcome that I want to achieve in each and every area of my life.

Now take a minute to make a list of five potential anchors that would remind you to look where you want to go.

After the minute is up, choose one of them and try this anchor for the next few days. This will be your powerful daily anchor for maximum focus.

If you feel good about it and you can see subtle changes in your con-centration and the outcomes you produce, stick with it.

If not, try another anchor from the list until you find your own unique anchor for your ultimate power focus.

He who has faith has an . . . inward reservoir of courage, hope,
confidence, calmness, and assuring trust that all will come out well.
—B. C. Forbes, founder of *Forbes* magazine

Points to Remember

The power, beauty, and simplicity of this rule is universal: "Look where
you want to go". This will take care of all the necessary adjustments
that need to be made in your life. There's no need to worry about it—it
will happen magically the more you focus on your destination.

Use a simple anchor, like a 1 written on the palm of your hand or
something similar, to remind you of the power and simplicity of this
rule and to shield you against making simple things complex.

Step 2

Embrace Yourself

Be One with Your Energy

Nobody realizes that some people expend
tremendous energy merely trying to be normal.
—Albert Camus

One of the hardest things in life is having
words in your heart that you can't utter.
—James Earl Jones

I had just finished one of my lectures at the Manchester Business
School and was stepping out into the hallway when a student from
India came up to me. "Tom," he said, "can I ask you a question?"

"Sure!" I answered. "Shoot."

"Do you have any advice for people to whom success doesn't
come easily?"

I looked at him, puzzled, and replied, "But I never said it was easy
for me."

And, unfortunately, it wasn't.

My Life as a Stutterer

My mind was drifting back to when I was 13.

I was sitting in class, and not a word would come out. The teacher looked at me and asked the same question again. I wanted to speak, the words began forming in my mind, air was blowing into my cheeks, but my mouth remained shut.

My abs were contracting, pumping, in a last desperate attempt to propel the words out, to open the dam, to let the waters flow.

But no.

I lowered my head in shame, with the whole class looking at me. There was silence—except for that inner pumping noise I was making.

The teacher understood, looked at someone else, and asked the question again.

Saved!

But the embarrassment remained and has stayed with me forever.

This gives you a brief look at what goes on in a stutterer's life each and every day. If you have ever been a stutterer, you know what I'm talking about.

There's the embarrassment and the shame. But most of all, there's your overwhelming desire to express yourself and the utter helplessness you feel when you cannot get the words out.

I still can't laugh at jokes about stutterers. I recently watched the movie *The King's Speech* on a plane. In this award-winning movie, Colin Firth plays an English king who is a heavy stutterer, but who has to give a speech to the nation that could be pivotal in deciding the country's future. I had to turn off the sound at a certain point; it was still too emotionally upsetting for me.

The life of a stutterer is not a life well lived—especially when you are a teenager.

People can be cruel. It's no fun.

But things got worse.

I developed severe nervous tics, first resulting in involuntary eye movements and then affecting my whole physical system.

My head and arms would turn uncontrollably at times, my facial muscles would twitch and contract on their own, turning my face into a wild grimace more often than not; and I couldn't walk properly.

Here I was: a bright, young, good-looking A student, a gifted dancer, and a multitalented scholar, but in a complete mess.

Let me tell you how I solved the problem.

When I was 16, I got a scholarship to attend a boarding school in the United States named Choate Rosemary Hall. Suddenly, sports was on the agenda every single day, for at least an hour and a half.

That was something new in my life. When I was growing up in Germany, sports were part of the curriculum just once or twice a week. Anything else was left to the students to organize by themselves in their spare time.

And I suddenly started to feel better.

It took me about two or three years to connect all the dots. But it was obvious.

The motor tics that were affecting my movements were the first to go. Then the stuttering stopped. I started to excel in languages, quickly becoming fluent in four and then five, from Italian and French to Portuguese. I became highly eloquent.

While I was still at boarding school, the first effects had already begun to show. I managed to join the public speaking class and got some of the highest accolades in the history of the school, even though I was a foreigner. I still remember rehearsing my speeches in the basement of my dorm, in front of the bathroom mirror, over and over again until my speech was flowing effortlessly.

I excelled in sports, too, after a while. The skinny guy who had always been among the last ones to be picked for any team at school reached a black belt level in Korean kung fu. I started to bulk up and played a wide range of sports. It wasn't long before I joined surfing competitions in Cape Town and was snowboard racing in the Swiss Alps, stand-up paddling along the shores of Maui with some of the biggest legends in the sport, and kitesurfing 15-foot waves around the planet.

The world was mine!

Trust in Yourself and Your Own Unique Energy

When Sylvester Stallone was a child, his mother was so bothered by his hyperactivity that she took him to a shrink. The shrink said: "There is nothing wrong with the kid, but maybe there is something wrong with the mother!"

As a child, I had always been hyperactive, but nobody realized it.

And, most important, neither did I.

Now not a day goes by without my doing at least an hour and a half of sports. My wife says it's as essential to my life as breathing. My assistant always puts those one and a half hours of sports into my schedule as an absolute baseline, no matter where I am in the world.

This has had a huge impact on my life. I've become a celebrated speaker, addressing past and present world leaders, billionaires, and celebrities around the globe. I've been invited to speak before leading political institutions like the European Parliament, have been filmed for documentaries as one of the leading visionaries of our time, and have been interviewed by preeminent financial institutions such as the World Bank. I'm a frequent lecturer at the best academic institutions and business schools in the world, from Manchester to Harvard, and am invited to speak regularly at cutting-edge corporations around the globe, from Interbrand and Puma to Google in Silicon Valley.

Linford Christie was hyperactive, and his teachers wanted to put him on medication. His parents refused, seeing his energy as a powerful force that needed to be harnessed. They made sure that his energy had a constructive outlet and gave him enough opportunity to do tons of sports every day. He became an Olympic gold medalist.

I remember the countless times my parents told me to "calm down" and "not be so nervous." My mother even tried to stop me from laughing out loud in the cinema until I felt ashamed of having so much energy and suppressed it even further.

In my early teens, my mother used to secretly slip herbal pills into my tea to suppress my energy. One night, I saw this strange, half-diluted pill lingering at the bottom of my glass, and I felt even more ashamed.

The Energy Inside You Has the Answer to All Your Problems

To accept yourself means to be *one* with your energy and the unique vitality of your body, to go with that energy and to trust that flow. And it will free you!

As I write in the section "Flip It!," there is a gift behind every major challenge or problem. You have to "flip it"—look at the other side of the coin. The energy behind your challenge, problem, or impediment is always good.

In my case, I was suppressing my energy, so it became stuck. And because I impeded it, it circulated inside of me and created all sorts of problems.

I realized that I had to do at least one and a half hours of sports every day. And when I did, the stuttering, nervous tics, and spasms vanished.

On a deeper level, though, this meant that I had to change my beliefs about my body and learn to *trust my energy* and surrender myself to it.

This way I could turn my physical problems into something constructive, creative, and beautiful. Once I just went with it and expressed my body's energy, it enabled me to speak several languages and express myself freely, write songs and perform them in front of thousands of people, become an accomplished athlete, and deliver gripping keynote addresses.

Once you express the energy and the unique vitality of your body, it will boost your productivity and performance in *all* areas. It will also create a true sense of well-being, happiness, fulfillment, and balance in your life. It can even help you, as it did me, to unlock the doors to hidden talents and skills that you never thought you had!

Exercise: Express Your Energy

Give Your Body the Room It Deserves

That's what Richard Branson, founder and chairman of the Virgin Group, said in reply to the question: "What advice do you have for people who want to become more productive?"

Richard added that it would give him at least four hours of additional productivity each day.

Time needed: 15 minutes, then as much as you need every day to have a true sense of well-being, happiness, fulfillment, balance, and productivity.

The first and most important question is: "Do you treat your body like a good friend, or rather like an enemy, a nuisance, or a pet that you have no use for?"

The next question is: "What would you need to do in order to give your body the full room it deserves?"

This includes exercise, diet, rest, sleep, and anything else that comes to your mind.

Then I want you to design a one-page action plan for the holistic well-being of your body. Do you need to arrange a meeting with a personal trainer or a nutritionist? Should you sign up at the local gym? It goes on your one-page plan. Have you always had a yearning to try yoga but have never given it room? What would be the next step—check out whether your nearest gym has a yoga class? What about sleep? Do you need an extra hour a night? Can you fit a power nap into your afternoon? What about your eating habits—do they need a makeover?

Don't confuse the holistic well-being of your body with outward appearance! I've met top models and fitness fanatics who looked great but were treating their bodies poorly, constantly depriving them of what they needed most and suppressing their natural impulses.

A word of caution: designing such a holistic plan and really taking an honest look at what your body needs will be a challenge for most people who are very "head-centered" and have to do a lot of mental work. They easily fall into the trap of thinking that the body is a tool to do their mental bidding, or that it's something that stands in the way of their goals. They see it as an enemy or a nuisance rather than a friend. In short, they think that their body's innate needs, desires, and energy stand in the way of their success.

Even my family laughed at me because they thought this young guy who's always stuttering in front of other people should be in front of 100 musicians and talk to them and leading them.
—Kurt Masur, conductor

Work out!
—Richard Branson

> ## Points to Remember
>
> Once you express the energy and unique vitality of your body, it will boost your productivity and performance in *all* areas. It will also create a true sense of well-being, happiness, fulfillment, and balance in your life. It can even help you unlock the doors to hidden talents and skills that you never thought you had!

Flip It!

Inside wants out.
—John Mayer

I prefer to distinguish ADD as attention abundance disorder. Everything is just so interesting . . . remarkably at the same time. Sometimes a person with ADD feels as if their mind is moving as fast as a speeding train.
—Francis Ford Coppola

I had never seen so many planes before. I was 16, and I was standing at JFK International Airport in New York City. I was a foreign exchange student, and it was my first time in the United States.

The bus had just dropped us all off at the wrong terminal.

What do you do when you barely speak English, you are alone with a bunch of other foreign students who know less English than you do, and you have all just missed your flights?

You concentrate like crazy. But then again, I had always been a good crisis manager.

A crisis had a beauty to it; suddenly all complex information, all possible variables, boiled down to one single next action. It required total focus and rapid decisions.

Like a kung fu fighter on water, I was now gliding from one move to the next. Everything around me froze into slow motion. While the others were stuck in analyzing the situation or getting into a downward spiral of desperation, I seized control.

I was able to find out where we had to go to get all our flights rebooked. I got all of us to another terminal. I worked with the ground staff to sort out the rebooking of all our flights, and we notified the host families that we would be late.

A few hours later, I was sitting in a tiny plane that was taking off to get me to Connecticut. The last thing I saw was one of my bags that had been left on the runway. Well, I didn't care. I was on the plane; that was all that mattered!

A Typical Moment in the Life of My Brain

Fast-forward to many years later. I have a million good ideas—and a few brilliant ones.

But being overwhelmed is my constant companion.

Music is playing in my head: Rachmaninoff, Billy Joel, Tiesto, David Guetta, Black Eyed Peas, Snoop Dogg, then Rachmaninoff again. Now a new song of my own begins to form, with lyrics rushing through and melodies flying. I dictate them into my iPhone.

Then there's an idea for my World Peace Foundation. Then another one for a new business I created. Then I feel a poem coming through and I have to capture it on paper.

Suddenly images start to develop and whirl around in my mind. I have an idea for an important meeting that's coming up in two days.

The Flip Side of Being Overwhelmed Is High Concentration!

For many years I had been struggling with being overwhelmed. I had had many coaches and the best time management experts. I had tried out every possible system, but I was just feeling more and more overwhelmed. My inner voice was crying out, "This is not for you!" but I ignored it. I was trying to fit into their system instead of designing a system that would uniquely suit my energy.

Then I had a breakthrough. I wondered: "What if I flipped the coin and looked at the other side?"

I had always had two major assets in planning and organization: the ability to brainstorm and create mind maps of huge size *and* the ability to know what was the one most important next action to take to move any of my projects to success.

Now I "flipped" it: they had been major assets all along. I just hadn't seen them as such because I was so focused on the problem that I impeded my own energy and power. I was looking at the wrong side of the coin. I saw being overwhelmed as a negative because I was not using my energy and skills correctly.

If you are good in basketball but you're lousy at swimming, you wouldn't hit the pool and conclude you're a failure at sports, right? Same here. I was simply looking the wrong way and following others rather than using my own intuition and my unique way of getting things done.

What's the flip side of being overwhelmed? High concentration.

Just as I had always been an excellent crisis manager and "conquistador of chaos," I could use the same techniques to filter the millions of pieces of information that were whirling around inside my head *and* the constant information overflow from the outside and thus create extraordinary success!

I got a sheet of paper and sketched out all the areas of my life, business and personal. I limited them to seven—the number that felt just right for me at the time to keep total focus and not become overwhelmed.

Then I designed my own system in which the next actions for all my priorities would always be on top.

I started to work from that sheet, and *bang*! I wasn't overwhelmed any more.

This way, I solved my own problem and turned it into a *mega* asset. I was now able to react swiftly to any changing environment and seize opportunities rapidly—just as I had done at JFK International Airport when I was 16.

The result: rapid decisions and fast success.

Most of Our Impediments Are Major Assets in Disguise

There is never time in the future in which we
will work out our salvation. The challenge is in the moment;
the time is always now.
—James Baldwin

The truth is, most of our impediments, problems, challenges, and even physical ailments *are* and *will always be* blessings and major assets in disguise. But as long as we label them as wrong, bad, or negative, we are stuck.

Again, let's remember the glass that's half full. You have to make a conscious decision to look at the glass as half *full*, not half *empty*, when you're assessing your skills, talents, and energy.

Ask yourself: "What is the energy *behind* my problem or challenge? How could that energy be used as a major asset rather than as an impediment?"

Life is trying to give you a present, but you have to unwrap it. It's that simple.

This will lead you to think differently, and you will discover your unique gifts.

Ingvar Kamprad, the Swedish founder and chairman of IKEA stores, said that he adapted the inner workings of his business to compensate for his ADHD and dyslexia. Richard Branson couldn't tell the difference between net and gross income, but he still managed to create the largest group of private companies in Europe by focusing on his unique talents and strengths as an entrepreneur and a visionary.

From Stuttering to Speaking Five Languages Fluently

In the section "Be One with Your Energy," I told you about my school life and my teenage years as a serious stutterer. I recall when I was sitting in class and not a word came out.

I was an A student with nervous tics and major physical impediments. Then I got a scholarship to attend a U.S. boarding school, and I had to do sports every afternoon.

This was when I discovered that I had always been hyperactive. As soon as I started to express my energy, my problems vanished.

My speech started to flow, and I learned to speak five languages fluently (not even counting my six years of Latin). My nervous tics and physical ailments disappeared. I was able to direct my energy and put it to constructive use. I became a black belt in Korean kung fu, started to surf big waves around the world with my buddies from Maui, went snowboard racing down the Austrian Alps, and excelled in stand-up paddle races in South Africa.

My parents, teachers, and peers had all taken the wrong approach by calling my energy bad. They saw the negative effects of the impeded energy and called the whole thing bad. They didn't look at the underlying positive energy that, once expressed, could be used most constructively to produce wonderful results.

Your Energy Is Always Good—Inside Wants Out

The basic assumption behind the solution is that your energy is always *good*!

What's there is good. If it's causing you problems, then you are impeding the underlying energy instead of identifying it as good and as a gift.

You are *sup*pressing it rather than *ex*pressing it.

I had to realize that the energy inside *wants* out. It's a gift that wants to be expressed, not suppressed. Then you can do wonderful and constructive things with it!

Throw away the boundaries of what people think is "normal." You will redefine what's normal and push the boundaries by living your own unique energy and individuality! That's what life is all about. Looking at the world, most people appear like zombies, unable to come alive. Wake up to your own energy!

In the same way that most failures are blessings in disguise, gifts that you have to unwrap, your personal challenges, impediments, or physical ailments are also gifts in disguise.

Your energy is divine. Take the red pill. Life is there for you to rock it!

EXERCISE: Flip It!

Time needed: 20 minutes

Society teaches us that we are "bad": we can't trust ourselves or our natural instincts, but instead have to suppress our energy and conform. That there are certain ways in which things are done, and that's it! That's bogus. Let's break through these limitations.

Take five minutes to identify an area of your life where you feel you are facing a major personal impediment, obstacle, or ailment. It's an area that constantly bugs you, the elephant in the room of your life!

This should be a difficulty, challenge, impediment, disease, or physical ailment that has been running like a thread through your life and that you clearly see as negative. There is no doubt in your mind that this is a big, ugly stone in your shoe that could not possibly have an upside.

Let's apply the "flip it!" thinking now.

Ask yourself: "What could be the underlying gift in this situation, challenge, or personal problem that I have to unwrap? What is the energy *behind* it that wants to be expressed but is being suppressed right now?"

To go back to my stuttering example, it was my hyperactivity that wanted to come out, the active physical energy that could be expressed beautifully in sports and language to produce outstanding results.

Then realize, just as I did, that the underlying energy of *your* personal problem, challenge, or impediment is *always good*!

Ponder that for a second.

The energy behind it is *always good*.

It's there for a *reason*.

Life wants you to express that energy rather than suppress it. If you suppress it, you turn it into a destructive force. There is no other way, and there has never been.

This might require some soul-searching, especially if your problem has been with you for a while. In my case, I was utterly convinced that my stuttering and my nervous tics were the most horrible thing in my life. I never even thought about flipping the coin to see whether there was another side, an upside, to my problem.

I've had people do this exercise who needed to go back to it a few times before they got to the bottom of things and discovered the major asset and upside behind their personal problem, challenge, or impediment. In particular, the longer you've been telling yourself that this is a bad thing in your life, the more persistence it will take for you to remove those mental limitations, look beyond the horizon of your existing beliefs, and flip your thinking.

For starters, give yourself 15 minutes to brainstorm about what the underlying positive energy of your problem, challenge, or ailment could be. This should include all the possible ways in which that energy could be put to constructive use.

My tip is to write down these possibilities on index cards, one by one. Then, after 15 minutes, take a good look at the stack of cards and see which one resonates with you most. Which one would you like to try on for size?

Take the smallest step: How could you act on this now? Could you schedule a time in your diary to give it a shot? Could you play with it a little?

Over the next weeks, go through the different ideas on the cards, try them out, and see which one produces the best results. This will rewire your brain and your belief system to turn the energy of your problem into a major asset.

The "aha" effect I've seen this exercise produce in people who've put it into practice has been truly life-changing for many of them. Have fun and prepare yourself for remarkable results!

> You take the blue pill, the story ends, you wake up in your bed
> and believe whatever you want to believe. You take the red pill, you
> stay in Wonderland, and I show you how deep the rabbit hole goes.
> —Morpheus, *The Matrix*

> No matter how thin you slice it, there will always be two sides.
> —Baruch Spinoza

Points to Remember

The underlying energy behind any major personal challenge, problem, or impediment, even a physical ailment, is *always good*! You have to "flip it"—look at the other side of the coin—and ask yourself: "What is the constructive energy behind this? How can I use this energy to my advantage? What is the underlying unique gift and blessing in this situation that I haven't seen?"

Then follow your own answers. This will turn your personal problem, challenge, or impediment into a major asset on your road to success.

Fun Leads to Your Greatest Successes

....

People rarely succeed unless they have fun in what they are doing.
—Dale Carnegie

I never did a day's work in my life. It was all fun.
—Thomas Edison

I just watched a famous German beer ad. A mechanic works hard all day, trying to fix an old car. Finally he reclines in a chair, opens a bottle of beer, smiles, and starts to drink.

Then it says: "First the work, then the fun." I had to laugh.

Like so many of us, I was brought up with the belief that you work your tail off first and the rewards come later, in some distant future.

"First the work, then the fun" means nothing other than "Work cannot be fun."

This detrimental belief pervades most societies. It's one of the biggest self-sabotaging deal breakers when it comes to your personal success, your life, your career, or your business.

The exact opposite is true: fun leads to the best results in all areas of your life.

If It Ain't Fun, Don't Sweat It! What the Prussians Got Wrong

Fun, fun, fun, fun, fun! Why do modern societies around the world have such a hard time with this? Growing up in Germany, I quickly realized that fun wasn't part of the game, *any* game that's played in Germany. And while Germans are good at engineering and mass production, they're not the happiest fellas in the world—or the most energetic or balanced bunch!

Real work is effortless. When you are having fun, you produce your best results.

We all know that when we are children, but we quickly lose that wisdom and that sense of ease and playfulness. We are taught that fun has nothing to do with work and getting results. We are taught that we produce the best results when we work *hard*. We are taught to go against our grain, against what we really want. We are taught not to follow our heart's desires and passions.

As a result, we end up going into careers that are hard work instead of fun. We are told to leave fun for some undefined later period in our lives and for hobbies.

Then we are so proud of ourselves for having managed to shove that fun-loving inner child aside and play society's game!

To Have Fun Means to Trust Your Energy

People are so afraid of having fun because having fun means trusting our energy. We are brought up to distrust ourselves. Fun is the most direct way in which our heart speaks out about what matters most to us.

On top of this, we tend to have a big distrust of effortlessness. Whatever comes about with ease is frowned upon. We are brought up with the belief that things that are fun are not really worth doing. It has to be *hard*! If you want to get anywhere, you need hard work!

For me, my Brazilian wife made a huge difference. She helped me to get into the Brazilian frame of mind, in which ease, effortlessness, and fun are part of everyday life. It's so ingrained in Brazilian culture that there can't be a day without fun. This also makes Brazilians a lot happier (besides turning them into great soccer players and their country into one of the biggest new economies in the world)!

Fun Is Your Guide to Your Greatest Opportunities

This was a major breakthrough for me. I have since come to realize that fun has always pointed to my greatest opportunities, my best meetings, and my biggest successes.

You can sense it ahead of time. The trips, meetings, phone calls, and projects you look forward to the most will produce the best results. The ones you dread, huuuh, are not good. In hindsight, they are often time wasters.

Fun is a great guide that can steer you fast to your greatest and most rewarding opportunities.

When I'm packing for a business trip and I'm looking forward to the trip with excitement and almost can't wait to go, it turns out to be a true winner.

Fun is your indicator of the best opportunities in your life, your career, or your business. Period.

It's your inner guidance system. It points the way to the most direct, easiest, and most joyful realization of your goals, dreams, visions, and plans.

If Richard Branson tells you to get people on board for your projects or business who are a "ball of fun," he means it. It's part of the secret success formula of all high achievers. This is why outstanding individuals across all areas, from business to philanthropy, from music to sports, are a load of fun to be around and have a great sense of humor.

Guess what struck me most when I first met Nobel laureates like Desmond Tutu or had my private audience with the Dalai Lama? Their great sense of humor.

Fun Points to Your Greatest Strengths

Fun also points the way to your greatest talents and strengths. Once you are doing what's fun, you naturally play to your strengths. Consequently, you will achieve much better results.

By doing what's fun and what you're best at, you will automatically replenish your energy and generate more drive to reach your goals. You will have much more energy available.

When I sit down to write; prepare a speech; get on the podium to speak, write, or make music; play with my band; go on stage; or meet exciting people to energize them for my world peace foundation, I am constantly refueling my energy. Sometimes I'm so "stoked" I can't even get to bed!

Fun will automatically lead you to what you love, and doing what you love will constantly refuel your energy.

You will only deplete your energy if you set yourself on a course where you consistently have to compromise what you love most.

Fun and talent go hand in hand.

If you honestly follow your fun, it will lead you to the full half part of the circle, namely, the areas where you're most gifted. At the same time, these will be the areas where you will make your biggest contribution to society, to humanity, and to this planet.

This will be the place where you will be most comfortable and where you will be rewarded with the most abundance in your life—not just cash, but well-being, fulfillment, and abundance in all its forms. This includes spiritual fulfillment, happiness, fulfilled relationships, and being with loved ones, family, and friends. It includes physical fitness, vigor and strength, and health and well-being. It means living and exploring your talents.

It also includes balance and a nourishment of your inner child. This inner child is amazed at the wonders of the universe and can't wait to get out of bed each morning and explore the magic of the day to make new and exciting discoveries.

Does this sound naïve and far-fetched?

This child is alive within you now, whether you realize it or not, and whether you're 8 or 80 years old.

Give it room. It wants to have fun and play!

Fun Leads to Success

"Fun leads to success." I put this on a big poster next to my desk, so that I could be reminded again and again of this beautiful yet simple truth.

Fun leads you to your "core genius." I was first introduced to the concept of the "core genius" by Jack Canfield, coauthor of the *Chicken Soup for the Soul* series. Your core genius is what you're best at, and your core genius leads to peak performance.

Fun is the magic key that unlocks all doors and all hidden potentials, and it comes with absolute ease and effortlessness.

EXERCISE: Trust Your Fun!

Time needed: 5 minutes

I want you to list everything that's fun; leave nothing out. Take a couple of minutes to put down everything you can think of, large or small, trivial or important.

Your Body

Then think of your most fun experiences and activities—the ones that make your smile become so wide that it has to be surgically removed, the ones that make your inner child proud.

What are the sensations in your body? Is anything that you feel, smell, or see more intense? Do you feel more *alive*?

Results

Now take a look at the results you achieve. What results do you produce when you're having the most fun?

Be honest with yourself. I'm sure you'll find that some of your greatest successes and achievements have come out of these periods of fun.

Catch Yourself

Try to catch yourself during the day when you stop yourself from having fun—when you think you've got to work *hard* to achieve anything worthwhile in your life, and when you're proud to feel depleted and exhausted from all this hard work.

Try to trace what's behind this behavior. Usually we follow this course because we believe it will lead to some imaginary big rewards later, or because we are just trying to fit in and get praise from others for working ourselves to death.

Remind yourself that fun leads to your biggest successes. The real work is done when your fun kicks in. That's when you're at your creative, professional, and personal best.

Next time you're stopping yourself dead in your tracks because you're having fun, don't stop.

Go for it!

Don't force your kids into sports. To this day,
my dad has never asked me to go play golf. I ask him.
It's the child's desire to play that matters, not the parent's
desire to have the child play. Fun. Keep it fun.
—Tiger Woods

Just play. Have fun. Enjoy the game.
—Michael Jordan

Points to Remember

Fun leads to your biggest successes. The real work is done when your fun kicks in. That's when you're at your creative, professional, and personal best.

Fun leads to the best results in all areas of your life.

Fun is the most direct way in which our heart speaks out about what matters most to us. Fun will automatically lead you to what you love, and doing what you love will constantly refuel your energy. Real work is effortless. When you are having fun, you produce your best results.

Fun is also a great guide that can steer you fast to the greatest and most rewarding opportunities in your life, career, or business. It's your inner guidance system. It points the way to the most direct, easiest, and most joyful realization of your goals, dreams, visions, and plans. The trips, meetings, phone calls, and projects you look forward to the most will produce the best results.

Fun also points the way to your greatest talents and strengths. Fun and talent go hand in hand. If you honestly follow your fun, it will lead you to the half-full part of the circle, namely the areas where you are most gifted. Once you are doing what's fun, you naturally play to your strengths. Consequently, you will achieve much better results. At the same time, these will be the areas where you will make your biggest contributions to society, humanity, and to this planet.

Fun is the magic key that unlocks all doors and all hidden potentials, and it comes with absolute ease and effortlessness.

Getting Things Right 51 Percent of the Time Is Enough: The Brazilian Surfer Meets the Monaco Millionaire

Certain flaws are necessary for the whole.
—Goethe

A professional is someone who can do his
best work when he doesn't feel like it.
—Alastair Cook, athlete

I was sitting with the father of one of my former assistants in the American Bar of the Hotel de Paris in Monaco. He was a Swedish self-made multimillionaire who had created his wealth by being one of the first entrepreneurs to import exotic fruits into mainland Europe.

He told me about his son's plans to start his own business by creating a men's clothing line. His son had told him: "Dad, I want to make everything perfect, get everything right." And his dad had told him: "To create success, you need to get things right 51 percent of the time, not 100. If you strive to be perfect in everything, you will wear yourself out and lose focus in your main areas or fail completely."

Fast forward. I was standing on Kite Beach in Maui, the most famous place on the planet to learn how to kitesurf. I was being taught by one of the riders of the Naish team, Paulo Franco, who is one of the best kiteboard instructors on the planet.

I was getting ready to launch. I launched the kite high in the air and the power of the wind lifted me a few feet off the ground, but then my feet touched the warm sand again.

I stared up at the kite and saw that the lines were tangled.

I looked at Paulo and shouted: "We gotta put it down again!"

But Paulo looked at me and said in his mild Brazilian accent: "No, you're fine; just go!"

And I screamed: "But the lines are tangled!" And he said: "Doesn't matter!"

I was getting nervous. Around me there was a whirlwind of kite-surfers coming into and out of the ocean on the tiny stretch of land, trying not to bump into each other. With all the guys launching and landing their kites, it was a challenge not to get their lines tangled into mine.

"But Paulo, you taught me that . . ."

"Go!" Paulo screamed. And I started to go for it.

I ran into the water, put the kite at two o'clock, let Paulo drag my body to the safe departure zone past the rocks, got into position, and put the kite at twelve o'clock right above my head. A split second later, I let it drop down in a beautiful S curve from left to right, way into the power zone—and took off!

The kite lifted me out of the water, and I was gliding over the blue ocean past a group of giant turtles.

The Naked Starlet Who Took a Bath in Champagne but Still Pulled Off a Master Performance

When I came back, Paulo shared his simple secret with me.

"You're German," he said, "and you Germans always try to get things perfect. When they are not perfect, you don't act. But sometimes in life, it's fine even if it's 51 percent. You gotta make sure you know which elements have to be perfect if you are to be able to take off, and which ones don't matter."

Wow!

Fast-forward to the Grand Prix in Monaco. I was standing on top of one of the biggest yachts in the harbor, and next to me was the son of one of the world's best-known billionaires and self-made entrepreneurs. With us was a famous young celebrity. (My only hint: she's named after a big city in France—you figure it out!) Admittedly, she doesn't have much of a brain, but with the help of her father and the world's best branding and image experts, she has managed to turn herself into one of the most recognized personality brands on the planet.

Wherever we went, the paparazzi lit up. The three of us had just spent a night at Jimmy'z, Monaco's premier nightclub, for Bono's birthday party and, to say the least, the whole weekend was unreal.

But what impressed me most was the impeccable professional attitude of the celebrity no-brainer. Whenever the cameras came out, she was ready. And I mean ready. She was the absolute consummate professional. Even with barely two hours of sleep and so much Crystal champagne in her blood that it would make Keith Richards look like a preschooler, she was as ready as if it were Oscar night.

Her personality: shallow. Her ethical and moral standards: questionable. But her professional attitude: impeccable!

She knew what to do for her brand and what she owed to her fans and, most of all, when to do it.

Her attention was barely there between her public appearances. She was almost a zombie on the yacht getting ready, at night after partying, in the VIP booth watching the race right across from the drivers' starting lane, and even in the Jacuzzi when she took off all that was left while she was getting soaked in champagne. But before hitting the cameras, it was makeup out, ready, smile, wave—go! She gave it 150 percent.

The lesson: be perfect where it counts. And get it 51 percent right the rest of the time.

EXERCISE: Be Perfect Only Where It Counts
Time needed: 5 minutes

Take any current project you have and spend the next five minutes trying to determine which elements are absolutely crucial and have to be executed perfectly in order for you to succeed, and which can be left to 51 percent.

A lot of us are born perfectionists; we place the bar way too high instead of clearly determining where it should be high and where it should be low enough so that we can jump over it with ease. If you are one of them, like me, you might say, "But they *all* need to be perfect."

Go back to the example of the starlet and remember her many downtimes of 51 percent and the few short peak performances in between when she gave it her all. That's why she is successful. She could never keep up that pace if she went for 100 percent *all* the time. Neither can you, and neither can I.

If you try to go for 100 percent all the time, you will invariably end up with 0 percent on a few critical items. And then your kite, project, idea, or business won't fly. You might even try to make this exercise perfect, but 51 percent is enough. That's why we have a deadline of five minutes.

Then return to your project, idea, job, or business and give yourself permission, just as Paulo did for me on Kite Beach, to let the wind blow in your sails and surf even though the 51 percent is only that: 51 percent. Remember: as long as you're surfing, you're good to go!

Gold cannot be pure, and people cannot be perfect.
—Chinese proverb

A good horse jumps only as high as it needs to.
—Persian proverb

> ### Points to Remember
>
> A lot of us are born perfectionists; we place the bar way too high instead of clearly determining where it should be high and where it should be low enough so that we can jump over it with ease.
>
> In any given job, project, task, or business, you have to make sure you know which elements have to be perfect if you are to be able to take off, and which ones don't matter. If you try to go for 100 percent all the time, you will invariably end up with 0 percent on a few critical items. And then your kite, project, idea, or business won't fly.
>
> Be perfect where it counts. And get it 51 percent right the rest of the time.

Embrace Your Laziness to Succeed

> Efficiency is intelligent laziness.
> —Anonymous

> An American of the present day reading his newspaper in a state
> of lazy collapse is one of the most perfect symbols of the
> triumph of quantity over quality that the world has yet seen.
> —Irving Babbitt

When I first stood in front of the MBA class and said the magic words, "You have to be lazy to succeed," I could see the sweat break out on the forehead of the MBA program director.

Most audiences are astounded when you talk about laziness. They're almost shocked, and definitely confused. This is especially true in business. People believe that success comes from hard work. Laziness doesn't fit into the puzzle.

In one of my later lectures at my Manchester Business School Leadership Circle, I took up the subject again. A student from China raised her hand and said: "But you still have to work!" Even after I explained to her about three times that I didn't recommend that she stop working, but simply that she incorporate a healthy portion of laziness into her life, she still didn't get it. She was so caught up in the belief system of constant production that you could sense her fear that if she let go for just a little, her whole world would come tumbling down—and success along with it.

Another student said, "But Tom, I feel I might be too lazy." I answered, "Then embrace your laziness as your unique key to success. When I did my master's in economics, there was a student who had started his own business and was studying at the same time. He devised a very clever system where he would never attend the lectures himself or do any of the reading. Instead, he would work with a fellow student who attended all the classes and did all the reading. This student would then give him a very concise overview and summary of all the material that had been covered. The result? He created a very successful business *and* finished at the top of his class at the same time!

"What that means is that you should embrace your laziness as a unique key that can help you find your own solutions, the ones that work for *you*. By doing that, you might just find solutions that can inspire others as well."

She was pleased. No one had ever told her that her laziness could actually be a good thing.

Balance and Letting the Light In

So what is it all about?

It's about individual balance. Incorporate a good, healthy portion of laziness into your schedule and your life. We live in a society of overactivity. Anything that is on its face unproductive, anything that is remotely passive, let alone lazy, is frowned upon. Yet it is precisely that unproductive inactivity that helps you produce the best results.

A good friend of mine, Rick Stack, an author, entrepreneur, and teacher, describes this as "letting the light in." Periods of inactivity allow you to tune in to your intuitive abilities; in modern terms, they will let you see the 5 to 15 percent of whatever you are doing that is really worth spending your time and energy on.

In short, you need maximum focus.

In economics, this is called the *Pareto principle*. Periods of laziness will allow you to apply that principle with a lot more efficiency because it will be a natural by-product of those periods.

Of course, there are still those among us who just "have to be busy." Trust me, having been born in Germany and raised there for the first 16 years of my life, I know what I'm talking about. Germans can't do lazy. It just doesn't work for their culture. They think overworking will produce the best results.

Well, if you are enjoying yourself *and* producing great results, fine. If not, reread this section every day.

Let the Artists Speak

> I tend to go through periods of idleness followed
> by periods of workaholic frenzy.
> —Stephen King

You probably wouldn't suspect that that quote is from someone who has written and published 49 novels and sold more than 350 million books, right?

Joaquin Phoenix, the musician, director, and Hollywood actor who was hailed for his performance as Johnny Cash in the movie *Walk the Line*, said that he would often just do nothing for long periods between roles. My take is that this is what puts him in a position to make his talent shine and go all out when he is on the set, which has earned him so many nominations and awards.

Philippe Starck is one of the most famous and most productive designers of our time. When it comes to designing an eclectic assortment of products, he has covered everything, from chairs and toothbrushes to restaurants and electric cars, from juicers and water cookers to hotel lobbies and megayachts. He says that his creativity is characterized by long periods of laziness and sudden bursts of inspiration, which then lead to his remarkable designs.

It took me a while to get out of my Germanic mindset. But by now my own greatest inspirations, songs, lyrics, and poems come to me during my laziest, most idle moments. I feel a sudden urge to write something down or record a tune in my iPhone. The lyrics to one of my favorite songs were born on an airplane while I was gazing at the sky, simply dreaming away. The words came out of thin air, the "invisible radio" that I describe in a later chapter, and I had to scribble them down. What was first a poem turned into the lyrics of a song that would go on to be featured on a famous album, travel the world, and receive millions of hits on YouTube.

What if You're Just Starting Out?

That's no excuse.

Let me take you to Marin County, California. I was strolling in the garden of Marc Allen's big white house on a hill. We had just played the piano together in his music room with its 15-foot ceiling. Now he pointed to the tennis and indoor squash courts at the far end of his property and said, "We use it for storage. I don't play." He smiled.

Marc was born in one of the poorest neighborhoods in the United States. He was still struggling to come up with $65 rent every month for his slum apartment when he was 30.

He later became the cofounder and owner of New World Library publishing house in the United States, the breeding ground for many *New York Times* bestsellers.

Marc is famous for never having worked more than 20 to 30 hours a week for his business, not even when he was starting his company.

He told me that preserving his ideal balance has put him in a position where he can recognize fantastic manuscripts when they come in. He shared the story of how he made a bestseller out of *The Power of Now*, by Eckhart Tolle. When it came in, Marc just knew that he had to publish it. He said he was holding the manuscript in his hands and just felt a unique opportunity, without even reading through it. The book later went on to become one of the bestselling books of the last 10 years and an international publishing phenomenon, selling several million copies in North America alone.

Had Marc been overworked, he would have missed it.

Laziness = Invention and Innovation

> A man is not idle because he is absorbed in thought.
> There is a visible labor and there is an invisible labor.
> —Victor Hugo

Periods of laziness put our minds into a state of free flow. Many great inventions were made by amateurs with a beginner's mind in that state because it naturally triggers those "aha" moments, as my friend Meng at Google puts it. Relaxation is the key to creativity and to finding the solutions you are looking for.

Most of the supersuccessful people I know—from Hollywood actors, world-famous artists, Silicon Valley executives, and CEOs who redefine their industry to the world's greatest entrepreneurs—make "laziness" and a load of fun activities a regular part of their lives. They work smart, not hard. They also spend enough time with their friends, their family, and nature.

But it's easy to get sidetracked and overwork—because everybody is doing it; because you are in debt; because you think you have to; because it's expected of you; because you are just starting out; because it's only temporary (the biggest lie!). And so on and so on.

Go back to the quote at the top of this section. Your goal should be quality, not quantity.

To reach your dreams, to have a balanced, fulfilled life, to have wild success, and to reach your ideal in every area of your life, you have to be both active *and* lazy.

Only then will you spot the unique opportunities that can bring the real quantum leaps and breakthroughs into your life.

What Exactly Does It Mean to Be Lazy?

I get this question a lot. It seems that we have forgotten what it means to be lazy. Not consciously thinking about anything, but just letting go, that's lazy.

There is no universal recipe for laziness. There's no one-size-fits-all. You have to follow your own natural inclinations; what is "lazy" to you might be "hyperactive" to someone else, and vice versa.

You have to go with your own energy on this one—as in so many cases. You have to trust your unique interpretation of what laziness means to *you*, and incorporate that into your life.

I'm hyperactive. Lying on a beach for three days straight would be pure torture for me. I would simply go insane. However, a few good hours of surfing, whether it's stand-up paddling, wave, or kitesurfing, can be "lazy" for me, as can dancing to Ibiza beats on my favorite beach, listening to my favorite music, cruising on my bike, or hanging out with my friends or family—laughing, cooking, and sharing stories.

It's your unique definition of laziness that counts. Whatever "lazy" means to you—*do it*!

EXERCISE: The Impossible Dream

Time needed: 2 minutes

For those of you who are having a hard time with laziness, we will ease you into it.

I want you to make a list of activities you would *love* to do but think you never have time for. Then select one and make an appointment with yourself to do exactly that during the upcoming week.

The Smallest Step

Again, I advocate the principle of the smallest step. Schedule the smallest possible amount of time for that activity in your calendar, even if it's just 20 or 30 minutes.

If you want to watch a movie, but you really can't push yourself to take one and a half hours, watch your favorite sitcom on iTunes for 20 minutes. If you want to swim in your local pool, but you really don't have an hour, go for 20 minutes. If you want to treat yourself to a spa, but you can't spare the extra dime or think you don't have the time for a full treatment, maybe a sauna session at your gym will do. If you would love to take a long walk outdoors but that time just never seems to come, maybe a 15-minute walk in the park around the corner will get you started.

Put your mind into a free flow during those times. Indulge in it! Have fun! Go wild!

Warning: don't turn trying to be lazy into hard work. There are those who make a job out of trying to be lazy. They go wild scribbling down all possible activities, then planning out their lazy periods to perfection. That's not being lazy, that's work!

And a final note: before you go on your field trip into the world of laziness, take a pen and paper with you. Your best ideas just might come when you're having a good time.

Points to Remember

Your goal should be quality, not quantity.

To reach your dreams, to have a balanced and fulfilled life, to have wild success, and to reach your ideal in every area of your life, you have to be both active *and* lazy. Only then will you spot the unique opportunities that can bring the real quantum leaps and breakthroughs into your life.

Incorporate a good, healthy portion of laziness into your schedule. It is precisely that unproductive inactivity that helps you produce the best results. It's your *unique* definition of laziness that counts. Whatever "lazy" means to you—*do it*!

It is the key to creativity and to finding the solutions you are looking for.

How to Do What You Love and End Up with More Time, Money, Focus, Energy, and Success in All Areas of Your Life

Genius is one percent inspiration and ninety-nine
percent perspiration. Accordingly, a "genius" is often merely
a talented person who has done all of his or her homework.
—Thomas Edison

My main focus is on my game.
—Tiger Woods

An important deal that I had been working on for six weeks had just fallen through. I had even postponed my summer vacation to work on it (never a good idea!).

I had lost time, money, and energy. But the very first thought that came to my mind was: "I could have used all this time to write, play the piano, or make music. And do what I love most!"

Your "Love Currency" and How It Can Help You Produce Outstanding Results

If you go straight for your goals, something magical happens. Suddenly your perception of time shifts. You measure everything in terms of your "love currency."

What does that mean? Let's go back to my example. I *love* to write music and make music. These are the absolute core genius areas of my life. They are what I need in order to be happy, and they are what makes me fulfilled. The time and energy I invest in my creativity, whether it's music or writing, automatically produce a higher focus, balance, well-being, success, happiness, wealth, time, and energy in *all* other areas of my life.

The more you do what you love, the more everything else will be measured in your love currency units. Every single moment you spend doing something else, you will be asking yourself: "How can I do this faster, delegate it more efficiently, produce better results, or team up with somebody so that I can have more time to do what I love?"

Even if you don't ask yourself this question, your subconscious will have begun to work on it. As a result, your perception of time will change. Your focus will soar. And you will concentrate on getting results fast.

Because of this greater concentration, you will go for it in everything else you are doing that is not your core genius. You will become more efficient at the things you cannot get rid of and still have to do, even though you don't love doing them.

Whenever we invest time and energy in doing what we love most, not only do we get it back many times over, but we invest in a power-house of energy and abundance.

Focus on What You Love—Everything Else Will Follow!

At some point, you might even become so proficient at this that you will find ways to complement yourself, team up with others, or delegate so that the things that you do not love will vanish completely from your life.

Does this sound naïve, unrealistic, and far-fetched? Then use it as an indicator that you still have a ways to go, and that this chapter is for you!

Almost all the high achievers and top performers in any field, fulfilled self-made entrepreneurs, and happy CEOs I know have been following and investing in their love currency consistently and ruthlessly from the start.

This *got* them where they are. This is where popular belief goes wrong. "Well, of course," a lot of people say, "*he* can do that because he's got enough time/money/resources/people/power/or whatever to do what he loves." Wrong!

These people got there precisely *because* they focused on what they loved most. This enabled them to get to the top of their field.

Where Do You Get Stoked?

Compare it to surfing. Once you start to surf, you love it, and you get stoked. You'll do anything to ride the next wave. That's simply all you care about once you are in the water. It's that ride, those few seconds that put a magic smile on your face.

You will be prepared to do anything for it. You don't care how cold the water is and the countless times you fall off the board. All the work you will have to do won't feel like "work" at all, because the ride is worth it.

It's the same in life. The more you do what you love, the more you will want to go back to it again and again. Every fiber in your body will yearn for it. The universe and your whole life will conspire to bring more of what you love into your life.

But the initial steps have to come from you. You have to take action.

Invest in yourself and take the necessary steps to make your core genius and what you love *the* central part of your life.

Then your core genius will produce focus, time, energy, and abundance in all areas of your life.

Start from the Inside Out, Not the Outside In!

A common mistake is to start from the outside in. Society teaches us to work from the outside in. Play it safe, work your tail off, then—someday, maybe—you'll get to do what you love.

If you start to work from the outside in, it means that you start with everything else that you think you have to do or should do before you finally get to what you love. You focus on getting everything else out of the way so that you will finally have the time and resources to do what matters most to you. Be careful! Don't make Plan B, C, or D your central focus.

Most of us are so afraid of failure that we become experts at anything *but* Plan A. Some of my German friends even start with Plan F and work their way up! That's insanity.

Remember: you get what you focus on. Devoting time and energy to what you love produces results, focus, and more of what you love—not the other way around.

Become a Master at Swimming Downstream

If you start by focusing on everything else in order to get the time, energy, or resources you need to do what you love, you will fail. Plenty of bitter people in retirement homes around the world are proof enough that this doesn't work.

It will drain you of your life energy, and you will end up with less and less of what truly matters in your life.

There is a simple truth at the bottom of this: our being naturally gravitates toward our core genius and what we love as the ideal natural state of our being. If we go against that, it's like swimming against a strong current. No wonder we feel so energy-drained, depressed, empty, frustrated, and disillusioned!

Unfortunately, we are taught from an early age to become great at swimming upstream.

What if I Have Become So Good at Denial That I Can't Find My Way Back to What I Love Most?

This is a great question, again coming from one of my global MBA students. He said: "Even in high school I already tried to excel in everything and be the best, no matter what. This was expected of me. I never questioned it. It got me where I am now, but I've completely lost track of what I love most. I don't know how to answer that question."

I was brought up in a family where the same was expected of me: be the best in everything, number one in *all*. I worked hard, and I was.

Was I happy? No! Was I steadily following what I loved most? Nope!

If you've been on the same path, then chances are you've become very good at *not* listening to what you love most. Instead, you play the "denial" game. Society is very good at teaching us that.

You have to unlearn this process and go back to your natural leanings, passions, and desires.

Life is *not* about being the best in everything and trying to please everyone. It's about pleasing yourself *first*. Ironically, when you do that, you're in the best position to help others and make your biggest and best contribution to society, humanity, and this planet.

Some of the other sections of this book will help you. But I recommend that you go at it from two different directions. First, write down your vision of your ideal future (discussed in another chapter). This will highlight what you are truly passionate about and where you really want to go.

Then go at it from the direction of your talents and strengths. Look at what you are really good at and what your natural talents are. Usually they become most apparent in your childhood or early teenage years.

What Are Your Three S's?

> I make sure I always go back to my three S's:
> the studio, the stage and the set.
> —Lil Wayne

On September 27, 2012, Lil Wayne passed Elvis Presley as the male singer with the most entries on the Billboard Hot 100 chart, with 109 songs.

This is why great artists who maintain their success over many years or even decades have learned to go back again and again to what they love, whether that means going into the studio, into their study, into their painting or writing room, or onto the stage. Even though they know that there are a million demands on their time, they go back to what they love again and again. Thus, they accumulate more energy, higher concentration, more focus, and greater abundance for everything else that still has to be done. At the same time, they achieve higher and higher levels of excellence in what they're best at.

This is true for writers like Stephen King and Paulo Coelho and for world-famous artists like will.i.am, Sting, Elton John, or the Rolling Stones.

Sadly enough, this is also the main reason that some amazing artists with promising careers get distracted once they are at the height of their fame. You never hear from them again. Did you ever ask yourself what happened to that awesome singer or band you liked so much? The one that had a smashing success but then disappeared into oblivion?

That's right, these people lose their focus and concentration. They get sidetracked into all kinds of projects, money issues, drugs, and every other possible distraction instead of going back again and again to their core focus.

What are your three S's?

It Is Never "Too Late"—There Are Only Solutions

This belief will cause you to focus on the solutions, rather than the problems or the challenges.

Write it in big capital letters on the top of a sheet of paper. Then, below it, write, "I have enough time to do what I love." Put the sheet in your folder and review it during your "Hour of Power" (discussed in a later chapter).

This is your insurance policy against the limiting beliefs that are reinforced by society everywhere: "I do not have enough time"; "Time flies"; "You can't do what you love"; "I'm too late"; "I'm too old to do that"; and so on.

Not true!

Time is what you make it. The belief that "there is no *too late*; there are only solutions" will empower you. It will change your perception of time, and this will change the opportunities that you attract; and these, in turn, will change your life.

The True Nature of Time

Time is a *flexible* concept, not a series of moments. We all know that as children, before we grow up and become clever and "educated."

Remember something fantastic that happened to you and that you truly enjoyed. This experience has stayed in your mind longer and is much more alive than other experiences. It enriches you and provides energy for everything else you are doing.

Think about the best foods you've ever eaten—the ones you remember 10 years and thousands of meals later. These experiences are "alive" now—you can still taste them.

The intensity of an experience determines its duration.

Consequently, time can be stretched by intensifying your experience, whether it's painful or joyful. In your best interest, let's go for the joyful ones!

My recommendation is: no detours! Stick to what you *love* and *blow it up*!

Make it occupy as much of your time as possible.

Free Drive

What happens if you let your mind go into a kind of free drive? We talk about this at length in other chapters. You discover whole new levels of solutions for your problems or challenges. You have those "aha" breakthrough moments.

You will also get a feel for and a glimpse of the true nature of time. Time will feel rather like something fluid, a giant ocean stretching out to eternity that is ready to bring you whatever you want!

It's your friend and your ally, not some crazy dog that you chase after. That's what most people do, however, especially if they're moving up the corporate ladder, starting their own business, or succumbing to some crazy work schedule that a burned-out boss has given them.

What If I Suck at What I Love?

We all do, at least at first. Except for the rarest of cases, such as Mozart, no one is born a great piano player. No one is born a great CEO, a great athlete, or a great entrepreneur, either. You're no exception.

But the love, the drive, the passion, and the desire will get you there. They will get you to greatness and excellence. They're your fuel, your rocket booster, and your greatest assets.

But at first we all look bad.

I'm always approached by a group of people after one of my concerts, and someone will say, "Tom, watching you play the piano, I wish I had continued to play when I was young."

And I always answer, "Yes, but you don't see the hundreds of hours I was practicing while the other kids were playing outside. If you don't have the passion or the burning desire to play, you won't get past the challenges and the countless hours of practice."

It's the same in any profession, sport, industry, or skill.

Your passion is the rocket fuel that will take you to the stars of your dreams.

Follow it. You don't need anything else.

EXERCISE: Do What You Love and Guard It at All Costs

Time needed: 10 minutes

Take five minutes, a sheet of paper, and a pen and draw a big circle. In the center of that circle, I want you to write your core genius and the activities that you truly love.

You don't have to make a full list. Write down the obvious ones, the ones that truly set you apart, your unique core genius and the activities that pop up as the central ones in the vision of your ideal future (discussed in another chapter).

Outside the circle, list all the distractions and demands on your time that usually pop up during a given day. These could be your kids, your current job if you are not doing what you love, or a lack of time, money, or resources—anything that has a negative effect on your following that core genius and devoting time and energy to what you truly love.

Again, this does not need to be a complete list. I want you to stop after five minutes. The whole point of the exercise is to recalibrate your brain and establish new neural pathways to safeguard that which is dearest to you.

Embrace Your Weaknesses

For the next step, I want you to become a little creative.

Take five more minutes, start at the top, go around the circle in a clockwise direction, and, next to each of the distractions, list one to three things that you could do to safeguard your core genius. In simple terms, how could you limit the negative impact of that distraction or demand on your time?

Brainstorm a little and come up with creative solutions. How could you offset the negative effect that this particular distraction or demand has?

Whom could you ask for help? Whom could you partner with to minimize the negative impact of that particular activity? Could you have somebody share in the profits from what you are doing? Could someone help you reduce your workload? What can you delegate? Could you ask your boss to team you up with people who complement you in the areas of your greatest weaknesses?

This takes guts. A lot of people in big organizations find talking about their weaknesses to be challenging. They feel that it puts their job at risk. As a result, they never rise to the top.

If this is a challenge for you, try to overcome that attitude. Don't listen to the voices in the back of your mind that have conditioned you to feel bad about what you lack most, whether it's your parents, teachers, professors, friends, boss, colleagues, or the media.

The whole point of this exercise is to help you find constructive ways to do more of what you love. Most of all, it is to help you affirm the belief within you that it is indeed possible to follow your true core genius and bliss.

High achievers in any area have come up with all sorts of practical solutions, lifestyle adjustments, game changers, and methods that allow them to devote a maximum of their time, attention, and energy to their core genius activities. The good news is: the more you do this, the more the wheel will spin in your direction, and the more valuable your love currency will become.

The result? Even higher focus, even higher efficiency, even better results, and even more time to do what you love. You'll have a happy smile on your face and well-being in all areas.

Surfing, alone among sports, generates laughter at its very
suggestion, and this is because it turns not a skill into an art,
but an inexplicable and useless urge into a vital way of life.
—Matt Warshaw, professional surfer

Points to Remember

The more you do what you love, the more everything else will be measured in your love currency units. Every single moment you spend doing something else, you will be asking yourself: "How can I do this faster, delegate it more efficiently, produce better results, or team up with somebody so that I can have more time to do what I love?"

High achievers in any area have come up with all sorts of practical solutions, lifestyle adjustments, game changers, and methods that allow them to devote a maximum of their time, attention, and energy to their core genius activities.

Invest in yourself and take the necessary steps to make your core genius and what you love *the* central part of your life. Then your core genius will produce focus, time, energy, and abundance in all areas of your life. The universe and your whole life will conspire to bring more of what you love into your life.

At first we all look bad. But the love, the drive, the passion, and the desire will get you there. Your passion is the rocket fuel that will take you to the stars of your dreams.

Time is what you make it. The belief that "there is no *too late*; there are only solutions" will empower you. It will change your perception of time, and this will change the opportunities that you attract, and these, in turn, will change your life.

Time is a *flexible* concept, not a series of moments. The intensity of an experience determines its duration.

Stick to what you *love* and *blow it up*! Make it occupy as much of your time as possible.

The Big-Wave Surfer Meets Google—
Use All Your Senses and Skyrocket to Success

> Surfing is like the mafia. Once you're in—
> you're in. There's no getting out!
> —Kelly Slater

> The best surfer out there is the one having the most fun.
> —Duke Kahanamoku

They were monsters.

I was staring at the waves that were crashing on the beach. Along with about 30 other surfers, I was admiring the biggest wave day of the year in Cape Town—and the three guys who were already out there taming the 20-foot giants.

I was scared, but I had a double espresso, called my wife, and went out there.

Looking back, this was one of the best days of my life. The intensity of the experience pushed me to the limits.

When you are caught in a 20-foot monster, you can't mess up. To pull it off and not get sucked into the biggest washing machine on the planet, I had to pump up the volume. I had to engage *all* my senses in a way I had never thought possible.

Once I went out there, I felt so alive. My senses became super sharp. The challenge forced me to use all of them to the max. It propelled me to another dimension of performance.

It was pure bliss.

The experience has stayed with me to this day. It has put me in a position to accomplish even greater athletic feats and to transfer this to all other areas of my life and business. It has allowed me to radically push the boundaries of what I thought possible in all other areas. Plus, the sharpness of my senses has allowed me to tune into my body as a tool to help me make the best decisions.

By nature, artists train themselves to be very receptive. A photographer is sensitive to light and its shades. A painter is sensitive to the form of an object. A sculptor is sensitive to touch. A musician is sensitive to sounds.

What can we learn from that?

The Big-Wave Surfer

People forget the benefits of tuning into your body.

When you are working your tail off, in whatever area, you usually dull your senses. You become very one-sided. Add to this living in a large city, and your senses become truly subdued. They lose their function.

This weakens your ability to make the right decisions and to act quickly on the spot.

Laird Hamilton is arguably one of the greatest watermen and big-wave surfers of all time, regularly defying what's possible. He's pushed the limits of the sport and surfed the biggest waves on the planet. For a quick two-minute overview, type "Laird Hamilton American Express Ad" into YouTube and prepare for an extraordinary ride.

In his book *Force of Nature*, Laird talks about the benefits of engaging and training all his senses to be ready for the moment when he's surfing down the face of a 30-foot wave at a speed of 60 mph. But what's in it for you? Why should you bother if you are not a surfer?

Training and engaging *all* your senses will prepare you to perform extremely well under pressure.

Google, Zen, and a Mind Like Water

A healthy mind in a healthy body: Google has certainly got that down.

To offset the heavy brain-centered work and allow people to rebalance and tune into their senses, Google offers its employees at its Silicon Valley headquarters free massages, lap pools, gyms, bikes, pool tables, and all sorts of physical activities. On top of that, it offers a program, run by my friend Meng, that is called "Search Inside Yourself" and teaches mindfulness—how to be fully present in the moment. Meng even turned it into a *New York Times* bestseller.

Training yourself to engage *all* your senses will allow you to do exactly that—to be fully present, operating at full capacity.

You will be able to read any given situation or person much better. You will develop a Zen quality of the mind where you can make instant decisions and react to any given environment and change on the spot. This is what the great kung fu masters refer to as "mind like water." It allows you to react fast to a changing environment, thereby reaching your full potential. Being fully present in the moment means that you have total focus. You are using your skills at an optimal level. This puts you in a much better position to tackle and solve sudden challenges that come up, in business *and* in life.

You will make your body an important decision-making tool that will give you the right clues when it comes to optimum performance, whether it's on the face of a giant monster wave or in your next sales pitch.

EXERCISE: Rediscover Your Lost Sense and Reclaim It

Time needed: 5 minutes

We typically don't train or develop all our senses equally. Usually one or two of them come up short.

I want you to rediscover your lost sense and reclaim it.

In my case, the most developed sense, by far, is my hearing. I can hear whole symphonies and songs in my mind, and rearrange them in whatever way I see fit. The least developed one is my sense of smell.

Now go through all your senses one by one (for the nerds, we have five!) and ask yourself: "Which is my most and which is my least developed sense?"

Then schedule a field trip in your diary to reclaim and rediscover that lost sense.

If it's smell that you need to reclaim, go to a perfume or fragrances store and try out the different scents. If you get the chance, watch the movie *The Perfume* to see how far that sense can take you and to expand your ideas of what's possible.

If it's hearing, try to detect even the faintest sounds in your environment. Get a full picture of the sound qualities around you. Whether you're in a big city or out on an open field of flowers, hold still for a moment. Close your eyes. Try to detect *all* the sounds. Take them *all* in.

Try this for a minute or two and you will already have opened the gates to a greater perception. Prepare yourself for an extraordinary ride!

When we're not operating in life-or-death situations, a lot of times we tune out. If you're sitting behind a desk all day, you don't have to be hyperaware. But it's important to exercise your instincts like you would a muscle. If you don't try to tune into everything—smell, hearing, sight, vibration—you can get dull, and that might come back to haunt you when it matters most.
—Laird Hamilton, big-wave surfer

Mens sana in corpore sano (a healthy mind in a healthy body).
—Latin proverb

Points to Remember

Reclaim your senses and use each and every one to the fullest.

The sharpness of your senses will enable you to read any given situation or person much better. You will develop a Zen quality of the mind where you can make instant decisions and react to any given environment and change on the spot. This is what the great kung fu masters refer to as the "mind like water." It allows you to react fast to a changing environment. Then you reach your full potential. Being fully present in the moment means that you have total focus. You are using your skills at an optimal level. This puts you in a much better position to tackle and solve sudden challenges that come up, in business *and* in life.

You will make your body an important decision-making tool that will give you the right clues when it comes to optimum performance, whether it's on the face of a giant monster wave or in your next sales pitch.

Your Happy Place—How to Find Paradise Wherever You Are and Turbocharge Your Energy

Be such a man, and live such a life, that if every man were such
as you, and every life a life like yours, this earth would be God's paradise.
—Phillips Brooks

I step out of the house, and there's an explosion of the senses. I open my arms. The scents of the hundreds of flowers around me mingle with the aroma of the ripe dates in the palm trees.

I feel a warm summer breeze, and the salty taste of the ocean touches my lips.

I sit down and glide my hand over a thyme bush. I close my eyes and take a deep breath. My chest expanding, nostrils opening wide, I take it all in.

One of nature's most sublime perfumes starts to fill my body until it pervades every cell.

It's paradise.

I open my eyes. The light of the hot Mediterranean sun blinds me and caresses my skin.

My eyes wander over the sailboats in the distance. I try to trace the different shades of blue in the ocean that keep rearranging themselves every day.

I cross the street and walk down to the water. My feet dig into the sand.

Suddenly I'm standing knee-deep in pure bliss.

I'm in heaven.

The Wall of Glass

Can you believe that I have ever walked out into that paradise without feeling a single thing?

Can you believe that someone could mess it up so badly?

Well, it has happened to me countless times.

You can be so caught up in your problems of the day that when beauty slaps you right in the face, you don't even realize it.

I call this the "wall of glass": you put up an imaginary wall of glass between you and whatever is going on around you. You shut down your senses.

"There's never nothing going on," Nick Nolte says in the movie *The Peaceful Warrior.* Yet you can make yourself immune to beauty, immune to life's wonders that are all around you, and drain yourself of the very energies that life has provided you with to propel you toward your goals.

We all need our daily dose of beauty—to recharge, to be at our creative best, and to get a step closer to creating and experiencing the most fulfilled reality we can.

I once had a terrific dream about how to get out of a very depressed state that I was in. It was simple: as much light as possible, as much interaction with others as possible, and indulging in the senses as much as possible.

Your "Happy Place" for Ultimate Power and a Turbo-recharge

How does that translate into optimum performance?

Indulging in the best that life has to offer and the natural beauty all around us leads to peak performance.

It promotes success with ease.

Wherever you live, there is a "happy place."

This will be the place you go to recharge and replenish your energies.

It's a place that you can visit daily, regularly, and with ease; that's close to where you live; and that presents you with an intensified sensory experience of what you love.

It's a natural energy booster that allows you to recharge your energies, gather your thoughts, and reach sudden breakthroughs—those "aha" moments—that come effortlessly and enable you to reach whole new levels of solutions.

What You Can Learn from Creative Artists

Artists do this all the time. We take a particular feeling or sensory experience, intensify it, and ride that feeling or experience to create works of art.

I want you to do something similar. Find your happy place, the place where you can intensify a pleasurable experience. Ideally, this should be a place where at least one of your preferred senses is maxed out.

You are unique. So is your happy place. It's not important that this works for anyone else. It has to work for *you*!

You might wonder: "How can I transfer that to my life if I don't live in a place as beautiful as the one you described?"

But you can find a happy place wherever you are.

It could be the Starbucks around the corner where you go for 15 minutes every morning to take in the smell of the coffee beans while you are waiting for your latte. It could be the flowers in the public garden close to the subway that you have to take every morning. It could be your own special spot in the library downtown. Maybe it's a little bench by the lake in Central Park where you can watch the birds flying over the glassy water. And for the CEOs, it just might be the pool in your backyard that you never use.

It's intensified pleasure; your own little safe haven; your own little paradise—just for you.

When you get back to work, this will allow you to see challenges in a new light, let you address problems with renewed energy, and give you a fresh outlook.

As an added benefit, life's unforeseen pleasures will reveal themselves to you more and more, even the ones you never knew existed. Someone once said, the organism should be an orgasm in motion. That's a great way to put it!

The Bigger the Problem or the Harder the Challenge, the More You Need Your Happy Place

The high achievers of this world make it a ritual to get in touch with their happy place on a daily basis.

At its headquarters in Silicon Valley, Google has created little islands where its employees can recharge, replenish their energies, and unfocus. There are arcade games, Ping-Pong tables, lap pools, miniature amusement parks, giant hulk puppets, little playgrounds, lounge areas—you name it. It's paradise. No wonder most college students want to work at Google. But it's more than that. Google's business model depends on constantly finding new sets of solutions and redefining the boundaries of what's possible.

Google has realized that the best creative work happens precisely when you are not aware of it—when you unfocus, relax, and don't think about the problem at hand.

The same is true for you, wherever you are, whatever you are doing, whatever your circumstances, and whatever organization you find yourself in. It's true whether you are the CEO or are just starting out, or whether you are a creative artist or an entrepreneur.

Your happy place will turbocharge your energy, help you perform better, and help you to reach those new levels of solutions that will skyrocket you to success.

EXERCISE: Find Your Happy Place—Wherever You Are

Time needed: 2 minutes

Make a list of five potential happy places close to your home. Then identify the one you will try this week. Schedule a date with yourself and your happy place in your diary. *Now*. Even if it's just for 15 minutes.

Then, over time, try to develop a habit, a ritual, of going there every day.

This works when you're on the road, too—whether you're an artist on tour or a businessman who needs to travel a lot. Once you've arrived, take 15 minutes to scout your new surroundings. Ask yourself: "Based on my usual preferences, what could be a good happy place for me here?"

Then develop a habit of spotting your happy place as soon as you get to a new location.

Points to Remember

Wherever you live, there is a "happy place." This will be the place you go to recharge and replenish your energies.

It's a place that you can visit daily, regularly, and with ease; that's close to where you live; and that presents you with an intensified sensory experience of what you love.

It's a natural energy booster that allows you not only to recharge your energies, but also to gather your thoughts and reach sudden breakthroughs—those "aha" moments—that come effortlessly and enable you to see whole new levels of solutions.

It will skyrocket you to success—a success with ease!

Step 3

Learn from the Masters

The Secret Success Formula: What Deepak Chopra, will.i.am, and Richard Branson Have in Common

I'm no genius but I'm smart in spots, and I stay around those spots.
—Warren Buffett

Know thyself.
—Ancient Greek aphorism inscribed in the
forecourt of the Temple of Apollo at Delphi

Like most of us, I was brought up in a society that taught me to watch out for my mistakes, flaws, and weaknesses. I was told that I had to work on improving in the areas where I was weak and that focusing on my strengths was not enough. Like so many people, I was made to feel ashamed of my mistakes and whatever I was bad at. I was told that if I wanted to get anywhere in life, I had to fix my weakest parts. Nothing could be further from the truth.

In the process of creating my biggest successes and in my work and interaction with some of the world's greatest leaders, outstanding entrepreneurs, Fortune 500 CEOs, self-made billionaires, Nobel laureates, multiplatinum Grammy Award–winning artists, leading philanthropists, and Silicon Valley megaminds, I have learned one thing: the exact opposite is true. Even if this lesson is the only one you take away from this book, your success will soar!

EXERCISE: Draw Your Own Circle of Power

Time needed: 6 minutes

This chapter is different from all the others because we will start with an exercise. I want you to take a sheet of paper and draw a big circle on it. Divide the circle into two halves, then color one half of the circle black and leave the other blank.

Now take three minutes to write your unique skills and strengths next to the full half of the circle. Choose the ones that come to mind most easily and that are the most obvious. The purpose of this exercise is not to make a complete list but to recalibrate your way of thinking and change your mindset. Now take another three minutes to write your weaknesses and flaws next to the empty half of the circle.

After you've done this exercise, I want you to take the following vow. Repeat after me: "From now on, I will never look at the empty half of the circle again. From now on, I will define myself and my unique contribution to this world, my self-esteem, my self-confidence, and my successes by looking at the full half of the circle. From now on, I will focus only on the full half and see to it that I strategically complement myself with the right kind of people to make up for my weaknesses in the empty half of the circle, people who are best at the things I lack most. I will never ever focus on the empty half of the circle again. By leading my life this way, I will achieve true greatness, reach my full potential, and produce my biggest and most enjoyable successes with ease."

Put Your Ideal Band Together

Let me ask you a simple question: if you had to put together a band, wouldn't you pick the best players of each instrument, not the worst, to make the music sound great? If you were the coach of a team, wouldn't you pick the best and most gifted players for each position? Yet most people look only at the empty half of their own circle of power. Because of their resulting low self-esteem, they never reach their goals, but instead waste their lives constantly trying to correct their weaknesses.

Don't Improve, Don't Fix—Complement!

Let me give you an example. One of my biggest weaknesses is planning and scheduling. If I try to do that myself, I tend to overload my schedule and my commitments. I don't have a real sense for what I can accomplish in a given day, year, or any other period. I overcommit, and so I become overwhelmed. Being overwhelmed leads to low satisfaction, low productivity, and a low quality of life. If I try to work this out on my own, at some point I become truly miserable, run around in circles, and don't achieve any kind of success that's worthwhile. So I have learned to complement myself with people who are outstanding at scheduling and planning and love to do just that. An entrepreneur friend of mine once said that for every weakness you have, there is someone else in this world who loves to do just that, is passionate about it, and does it well. Well said.

Meet Richard Branson

Richard Branson is a prime example of not focusing on what other people would call weaknesses. He didn't even put them in the half-empty part of the circle. He saw them instead as assets and put them in the half-full part. Being faced with dyslexia and ADD, Richard said, forced him to focus on the most essential things in each area and to get to the bottom of everything fast and efficiently. In short, it forced him to concentrate on what really mattered. As the Greek saying goes, "Know yourself," and that knowledge lies exactly in the half-full part of the circle.

Don't Waste Your Time Trying to Turn Your Weaknesses into Strengths

The biggest obstacle is the belief and mindset that you have to turn your weaknesses into strengths. As Richard Branson said, nobody will ever remember you for your weaknesses, because even if you try to improve them, at best you will become mediocre in those areas; you will never be outstanding. Let's look at your circle again. For everything that you've written next to the half-empty part of the circle, there's someone who loves to do just that and is brilliant at it. Your task is to go out and find these people. Complement yourself with people with just the right skill sets so that you can focus on your core genius and make it shine. Your core genius is what you're best at and where you make your biggest contribution at the same time—to yourself, to humanity, and to the world at large. It's also the one and only way to produce your biggest successes with ease.

Meet Deepak Chopra

Any outstanding leader and highly successful person I know is applying the principle of focusing on the half-full part of the circle. Life has already dealt you the right cards to make you a winner! There is an innate order to things that comes into play once you take that half-full part of the circle and concentrate on it. By complementing yourself with the right people in all areas, either by employing them as staff members, teaming up with them, or working in partnership with them, you automatically put the people you're working or cooperating with in their best positions. They too can focus on their unique strengths and skill sets, their talents, and everything that's in their half-full part of the circle. Meet Deepak Chopra, a friend of mine and a global advisor of my World Peace Foundation. Deepak is a worldwide bestselling author, an outstanding meditation teacher, the founder of the Chopra Foundation, and a world thought leader across generations. He is an inspiration to watch. He clings exclusively to what he does best and loves to do. He has complemented himself with just the right people in all areas so that he can continue to focus on his core genius each and every day of his life. Consequently, he makes the best contribution to himself, his own life, the people around him, humanity, and this planet by doing what he does best. For him, this is writing books, speaking, teaching, leading workshops and retreats, bringing thought leaders together, and inspiring people around the globe daily using various forms of social media and cutting-edge technologies. He focuses on getting his key unique messages across to heal people, put humanity and the world in balance, and improve our state of *well-being*, his favorite word. He has people who take care of his schedule, of organizational and business matters, and really of everything that he doesn't want to concern himself with personally.

Meet will.i.am, Modern Pop Icon and Global Superstar

Will.i.am is a Grammy Award–winning, multiplatinum artist, singer, songwriter, philanthropist, and entrepreneur. With him as front man, the band Black Eyed Peas has sold more albums in the last five years than any other band on this planet. Will is also a true pleasure to watch when he's in action.

He has a lot of staff because of the many different projects he's involved in, from his own foundation and his music and acting career to becoming an idea generator for the world's biggest brands, from Coca-Cola to Intel. He has to delegate things in each and every area of his life ruthlessly. Anything that doesn't pertain to his core strengths and his genius is delegated to someone else who does just that and is brilliant at it. When I was in the trailer with will.i.am and the key members of his staff just before he went on stage with Black Eyed Peas at the Apollo in New York City, it was like a well-oiled military machine. All the ducks were lined up in a row: his agent; his lawyer; the women running his foundation, "I Am Angel"; his personal manager, Polo; and the rest. Each and every one of them had his or her own unique place in the setup, doing exactly the thing that he or she was most capable of. It reminded me of a comment the manager of the rock group U2 once made in a private conversation: "The U2 world tour is like a military operation." Consequently, will.i.am has become one of the most recognizable faces in modern entertainment and has been called one of the symbols of the future of entertainment by President Obama.

In Short, Delegate Ruthlessly!

Your core genius should also be the area where you spend most of your time. In Will's case, this is either the studio, the stage, or some other creative setup where he can concentrate on his creativity and his performance abilities. Doing anything that doesn't pertain to one of these three S's would take time away from his core activities and consequently wouldn't contribute to producing his biggest successes. This is why he delegates ruthlessly—so that he can spend his time where it matters most, even if that's Intel's boardroom.

Ruthless delegation is the key concept. And yes, you have to let go of perfectionism when you delegate. I still remember my first phone call with Richard Branson, my first phone call with Deepak Chopra, and my first meeting with will.i.am. They work in totally different fields and industries, but all three of them share the same success formula and habits. They take decisions superfast. They delegate instantly. A meeting or phone call with any one of them might not take longer than five minutes, but it could kick off three different projects.

Make it a personal goal to get to that level of excellence where you can decide upon and delegate everything in five minutes.

Points to Remember

Society teaches us that if we want to get anywhere in life, we have to work on improving in the areas where we are weak. High achievers from all areas show us that the exact opposite is true. They focus only on the half-full part of their circle of power, namely, their unique talents and strengths. They strategically complement themselves with the right kind of people to make up for their weaknesses in the empty half of the circle, the ones who are best at what they lack most.

By leading life this way, they achieve true greatness, reach their full potential, and produce their biggest and most enjoyable successes with ease. At the same time, this places them in a position where they can make their best contributions to society and to the world at large.

The Champion's Attitude—The Secret of the Ones Who Finish First

It's a question of who believes and who wants it more.
Which player is mentally stronger? Which player is going to
fight the hardest in the big points? These are the things
that determine who is the champion.
—Novak Djokovic, Serbian tennis player

I was sweating like hell.

I kept focusing on Holger's eyes as we circled each other.

Our hands, heads, and legs were covered in protective gear to soften the heavy blows.

Out of the corner of my eye, I sensed the three masters kneeling on the ground, watching my every move from the far end of the room.

There was silence, a moment of vacuum.

Then a series of yup-chagis came raining down on me, side kicks to the head. The fight was on in the final battle for my black belt in Korean kung fu.

After the fight, my master came to me and taught me one of the most valuable lessons of my life: the Champion's Attitude.

"You know, Tom, I can sense at the beginning of a fight who will win. The winner has a calmness in his eyes, a sense of knowing that he will win. This attitude, this expectation, becomes a self-fulfilling prophecy."

If You Expect Something to Happen, It Will Happen

One of my best friends, Bernard Lambert, has been a mind-body coach to many athletes, including bodybuilding champions and Olympic gold medalists, and to Hollywood actors and famous singers. He is 69, but looks 20 years younger and has the body of a well-trained 30-year-old (no kidding!), including the six-pack abs.

Bernard also says that he can detect a champion right away, and he has taught me a lot about expectation. The calmness in the winner's eyes comes from the self-taught expectation of success. It's an inner knowing, a sense of total clarity.

I later had a dream in which I was doing front handsprings effortlessly, a move that I had always wanted to master. In the dream, I heard a voice say: "If you *expect* something to happen, then it *will* happen. The ease, the effortlessness is what's important."

And I finally got it!

If you expect it to happen, then it will happen. As soon as you start to focus on your worries, fears, or doubts, you will fail.

You can use suggestion to hypnotize yourself into believing and expecting that you will succeed, and that whatever event you want to create or goal you want to reach will materialize.

Then what you want to have happen will actually happen with such ease that it will surprise you.

Remember, it's *all* in the mind. If you expect something to happen, then it *will* happen.

Tunnel Vision

Arnold Schwarzenegger calls this "tunnel vision": you focus on the mental image of what you want to accomplish, then you hold that image in your mind at all costs, wherever you are and whatever you do. If you want to become the mayor of your town, that's the image you focus on in your mind. If your goal is to become the next leader in your field of business, that's your focus.

You block out everything else. You expect that you will achieve it, and you concentrate on it until there is no doubt in your mind that you will achieve your goal.

When he first came to the United States from his small village in Austria and talked to Joe Weider, the father of bodybuilding, Arnold predicted that he would become the best bodybuilder in the world, then become a top actor, and then go into politics. He accomplished all three.

Later, Arnold often talked about the importance of having a tunnel vision and the key role this vision played in enabling him to reach his goals. He stressed how important it was to focus on your goal at all times, single-mindedly, until your mind accepts as a fact the idea that you will reach it, no matter what.

Whenever I have applied the Champion's Attitude in my life, this attitude of expectation has always drawn the events that I strongly desire to me. This works in any area, from sports, philanthropy, and business to entrepreneurship, innovation, and creativity—you name it.

Of course, the contrary is also true. If you focus on your fears, worries, or doubts, that's what you will attract.

EXERCISE: Remember the Champion in You

Time needed: 5 minutes

Once again, use your past as a rich source. Search it for your biggest successes.

Then try to detect how you applied a Champion's Attitude in those episodes and what outcome it produced. When were you so convinced that you could not fail that you actually accomplished your goal with ease?

EXERCISE: The Sandwich Technique

Time needed: 5 minutes

Make it a ritual to look back at your day and your biggest successes before you fall asleep.

Use the sandwich technique. First think of a success and how you helped to bring it about by having a Champion's Attitude. Then try to spot an event in your past that you strongly desired and cared deeply about, but just couldn't pull off. Try to be honest with yourself about your expectations surrounding that event. Were you truly convinced? Did you have a Champion's Attitude?

Now think back to another positive experience in your life where you produced great success and see if you can spot your Champion's Attitude again.

EXERCISE: The Magic Trigger

Use a visual trigger to remind yourself of the importance of the Champion's Attitude in drawing whatever you desire into your life. I personally keep a silver bracelet on my right wrist that was given to me by one of my best friends after I pulled off the inaugural World Peace Festival. It's a constant visual reminder that I can accomplish whatever I put my mind to, and that my expectation is key.

Whenever you look at your trigger, give yourself the following suggestion: "It's going to happen—no matter what!"

A sense of calm, relaxation, inner peace, clarity, and knowing that you *will* succeed are signs that you are on the right course, and that the trigger you have chosen for yourself actually works.

Watch how that trigger helps you to develop a Champion's Attitude of strong expectation as it draws the events you desire into your life.

You gotta get up and say: "I wanna be a champion!"
and do whatever it takes. If you don't see it or
believe you will be a champion, who else will?
—Arnold Schwarzenegger

For me, I'm focused on what I want to do. I know what I
need to do to be a champion, so I'm working on it.
—Usain Bolt, Jamaican sprinter

Points to Remember

Apply the Champion's Attitude to reach any goal you strongly desire in business and in life. If you *expect* something to happen, then it *will* happen! This attitude, this expectation, becomes a self-fulfilling prophecy.

Remember the ease, the effortlessness. It's *all* in the mind.

You can use suggestion and visual triggers to hypnotize yourself into believing and expecting that you will succeed and that the event or goal that you want to materialize will happen.

Remind yourself of the importance of having tunnel vision. Focus your view on your goal, single-mindedly, until your mind accepts as a fact the idea that you will reach that goal—no matter what.

The contrary is also true: if you focus on your fears, worries, or doubts, that's what you will attract.

Expect it to happen! Then it will actually happen with such ease that it will surprise you.

The Golden Rule: What the Dalai Lama Taught Me About Energy

> Energy cannot be created or destroyed, it can only
> be changed from one form to another.
> —Albert Einstein

> In times of great stress or adversity, it's always best to keep busy,
> to plow your anger and your energy into something constructive.
> —Lee Iacocca

I was in a big hotel in Memphis, and the bomb squad was surrounding the whole building. Police were everywhere.

I was getting ready for my private audience with the Dalai Lama—not a simple, everyday meeting. I passed about 15 bodyguards and finally got to a huge Secret Service guy in front of the door to the Dalai Lama's suite. He asked me: "A lot of people would either kill or pay a lot of money to go through this door. What have you done to receive such an honor?" I smiled.

The Dalai Lama took me by the hand in his simple, jovial, and down-to-earth style, as if we had known each other since childhood. He led me to the sofa, and we sat down.

One of the things I learned from him that really impressed me was how to deal with energy. "Whenever something upsetting or tragic happens," he said, "we try to go about it in the following way: If we can change it, then we focus our energy on changing it. If we cannot change it, then there's no use worrying about it, either. Then we had better concentrate our energy somewhere else."

The basic truths are simple, and so is this one.

The simplicity of this rule will be life-changing once you actually apply it and don't just brush it off as a nice anecdote.

Energy Is Energy

Energy is energy. It's up to you to decide what to do with it and where to direct it. What if something bad and unexpected happens? Use the energy to create something constructive.

How often do we get caught up in the daily nonsense we have to deal with and let ourselves get entangled in worries or focus on the negative? Instead of focusing on what we really want and channeling our energy in the best way, as the Dalai Lama described, we focus our thoughts and actions on all the things in the past or the present that we cannot change or on everything we don't want to happen in the future.

I've since tried to apply the Dalai Lama's rule to a lot of different situations in my life, with amazing results, and have passed it on to others as often as I could.

I grew up in Germany, and Germans certainly do their fair share of worrying and impeding their energy. They usually focus on what they dislike and spend most of their day talking about it.

Applying the Dalai Lama's rule would make Germany a much happier place. But this problem is not confined to Germany. Don't we all fall into this trap of succumbing to the negative news—of getting caught up in the headlines of the day, however negative they might be, instead of focusing on the joys, the magic, and the beauty of living?

Instead of channeling our energy in the most constructive manner, we often focus on or worry about things that we cannot change. This is not working, and we know it. Why do we still make this a golden rule of our day? Because society, our educational system, the news, and everything that we're bombarded with on an everyday basis have conditioned us to believe that this is the best way to do things. They constantly reinforce a belief in negativity and a concentration on lack, scarcity, and limitation.

Furthermore, we are brought up to worry and with the basic belief that the more we actually concentrate on a problem, the more likely we are to solve it. The opposite is true.

EXERCISE: The Dalai Lama's Rule in Action Can Reclaim Your Infinite Power and Seize the Magic of the Moment

Time needed: 30 seconds

Whenever something upsetting or tragic happens, apply the Dalai Lama's rule: If you can change it, then focus your energy on changing it. If you cannot change it, then there's no use worrying about it. You should concentrate your energy somewhere else.

That sounds simple, but it's challenging in practice, since we are conditioned to do exactly the opposite.

You will have to remind yourself again and again not to fall into this trap.

During the day, try to catch yourself whenever you are going against the Dalai Lama's rule. Try to detect the beginnings of the mental downward spiral of channeling your energy in an unconstructive manner by worrying about or focusing on the things you cannot change.

Then make a snapping gesture with your hand to serve as a mental trigger to snap you out of this state. It will also serve as a reminder that you can actually get out of it in a second; it takes no more. It's simply a mental switch.

You have the power to focus on whatever you want and to channel your energy in whatever direction you choose.

EXERCISE: Count Your Blessings

Time needed: 30 seconds

Just the simple fact that we wake up alive every morning is a blessing in itself.

How many of us ever get up and count our blessings? How much do we express gratitude? I try to make it a rule to do so. Whenever I get up in the morning, I count 10 fingers of gratitude. I try to list 10 things I am grateful for, large or small, in no particular order. This gets me to refocus on the half-full part of the glass and on the opportunities, the endless possibilities, and the good things in my life.

So I suggest that you try this simple experiment. Whenever you get up in the morning, try the 10-finger exercise of counting your blessings. Again, it doesn't matter whether they are large or small or whether you just express gratitude for being alive. I'm sure you'll easily find nine other things you're grateful for.

Don't get caught up in the mental trap of feeling that if you haven't accomplished the big things in your life, you have nothing to be grateful for. The key is to be grateful for the simple things, the things we too often take for granted. Whether it's people surrounding us with love, the flowers in our garden, the sun that wakes us up in the morning, health or abundance in whatever area, or the talents and skills we have—however insignificant these things might seem, they all contribute to the beauty of our being and to our state of joy and bliss.

We have to cultivate that state. The simple 10-finger rule will get you into that frame of mind.

Feeling sorry for yourself and your present condition is not only
a waste of energy but the worst habit you could possibly have.
—Dale Carnegie

In times of great stress or adversity, it´s always best to keep busy,
to plow your anger and your energy into something constructive.
—Lee Iacocca

Points to Remember

Energy is energy. It's up to you to decide what to do with it and where to direct it.

What if problems crop up? Use the energy to create something constructive.

Whenever something upsetting or tragic happens, apply the Dalai Lama's rule: If you can change it, then focus your energy on changing it. If you cannot change it, then there's no use worrying about it. You should concentrate your energy somewhere else.

The simplicity of this rule will be life-changing once you actually apply it.

Role Models

The wonderful things in life are the things you do, not the things you have.
—Reinhold Messner, adventurer and explorer

Success leaves clues.
—Tony Robbins

When Arnold Schwarzenegger was growing up, he was in big trouble.

Born and raised in a little village in Austria, he had plastered the walls of his room with images of muscular men in tiny bathing shorts in eye-catching colors. His parents called the family doctor (there were no shrinks in rural Austria at that time!). The doctor came to the house to see if there was something "wrong" with the boy.

After having examined Arnold, he told the boy's mother: "Listen, there's nothing wrong with the kid; he's just very, very ambitious."

Who Is Your Role Model?

You may say whatever you want about Arnold, but he is certainly one of the greatest goal setters of all time. Before he came to the United States, he had already carved out a plan. First, he was going to make it big in bodybuilding, but not only big: he was going to become the biggest bodybuilder of all time. Then he was going to go into the movies, and then into politics. He even predicted that he would marry a Kennedy.

We know that all of this came true.

He certainly had everything going against him, from his upbringing to his accent, to the way bodybuilders were perceived in Hollywood, to loads of other misconceptions, prejudices, and limiting beliefs that he was going up against.

But he was dead set on his goals, and that was all that mattered. On his way to his successes, Arnold constantly surrounded himself with the images of his role models. Kids do this all the time. But when we "grow up" and become adults, we think it's foolish to plaster our walls with images of role models that we want to emulate.

In his great book *Rich Dad, Poor Dad*, Robert Kiyosaki describes how he constantly uses role models in whatever he does to get better results and improve his skills. When he's on the golf course, he pretends to be Jack Nicklaus or Tiger Woods. When he's engaged in a deal, he pretends that he's Donald Trump. When he tackles anything to do with investing or finances, he pretends that he's Warren Buffett.

All the great inventors, artists, businessmen, and athletes of our time use role models to inspire them and to help them push the boundaries of whatever they think is possible.

Today, it's easier than ever before to find out everything about the role models who truly motivate you to reach the stars and your greatest potential. "The web is the biggest library in the world, and it's always open," my fellow Club of Budapest member Paulo Coelho likes to say. It gives you unlimited access to the role models who really inspire you and lets you zoom in on them 24/7.

Success Leaves Clues

When you tune in to your role models, a fantastic phenomenon kicks in: you begin to acquire some of their skill sets.

As soon as you focus on someone intensively and over time, you tune into that person's worldview.

This means that you actually start to copy his or her belief systems and can then apply those systems to any activity or skill in your life, career, or business.

This is a fantastic tool that life presents us with! It's paradise.

Even if you have no education and no prior experience in whatever it is you are setting out to accomplish, you can tune in to your role models. Suggest to yourself that you will model their worldview and skill sets. This way, you can copy their beneficial and constructive traits even faster. It's like a giant supermarket where you can literally choose and pick what you want to become.

It's Your Focus and Willpower That Count—
Not Your Genetics, Heritage, or Background

Reinhold Messner is arguably the greatest mountaineer of our time. He has broken all records and was the first person to climb Mount Everest without supplemental oxygen. He was also the first person to ascend all 14 "eight-thousanders" (peaks higher than 8,000 meters or 26,000 feet) in the world.

Doctors examined him to find out what made his body so special that he could do the seemingly impossible and accomplish physical feats that no other human being had ever pulled off. They found a shocking truth: he was totally average. His genetics had dealt him no upper hand when it came to his physical abilities.

What he had, however, was an immense power of the mind, a focus and concentration and unwavering willpower. This was what really set him apart.

The same goes for you. Whatever you are setting out to do, whatever you want to be or have, or whoever you want to become, you *can* do it.

You can even push the boundaries of what the world of today thinks is possible, whether you're an athlete, a businessman, an entrepreneur, somebody working in a nongovernmental organization, an artist, or a student.

You can make us all realize that there is more out there. You can show us the true potential of what we all can accomplish by growing beyond what anyone else has ever done.

As we discuss in another chapter, any information you want *is* available to you if you focus on it. Your desire will draw it to you. The same thing is at play here: you start to acquire the skill set of your role model by focusing on those skills with enough passion and desire.

This way, you create a powerful magnetic force that will draw to you the skills and belief systems that you need in order to reach your goals.

This force will make you adapt in the best way possible so that you can soar to unexpected heights, reach your dreams, acquire and display the same characteristics, and even go beyond what your role model has accomplished. In the end, as with everything in life, you are limited only by what you believe is possible.

Like a magic sponge, you will draw the information you need to you and adapt it to your personality. That's the power of the mind that our scientists have only begun to scratch the surface of.

EXERCISE: Pick One!

Time needed: 3 minutes

Take the one area of your life that you are least pleased with and that you most want to improve.

Then pick a role model for this area.

Go on the web and search for inspiring images or videos about your role model that you can save on your desktop or on your smartphone.

Then make a ritual of looking at these images or videos every morning after you get up (I personally use a mixture of pictures and videos). While you are doing this, tell yourself: "I am now tuning into the worldview of . . . ," and fill in the blank.

Do this every morning until you see amazing results!

Points to Remember

All the great inventors, artists, businessmen, and athletes of our time use role models to inspire them and to help them push the boundaries of whatever they think is possible.

Constantly surround yourself with the images of your role models. As soon as you focus on someone intensively and over time, you tune in to that person's worldview.

When you tune in to your role models, a fantastic phenomenon kicks in: you create a powerful magnetic force that will draw to you the skill sets and belief systems that you need in order to reach your goals.

How to Exude Self-Confidence and Charisma Wherever You Go: Tips, Tricks, and Best Practices

Believe in yourself! Have faith in your abilities!
Without a humble but reasonable confidence in your own
powers you cannot be successful or happy!
—Norman Vincent Peale

Confidence is the greatest friend.
—Lao Tzu

I was sitting in the living room with my parents. They had their adopted grandchild over, a girl who still has that natural purity and amazing spontaneity that slap you right in the face.

She had just completed a 200-piece puzzle that was designed for children twice her age. She looked at me, threw her arms in the air, and exclaimed: "I'm a genius! I'm a genius!"

The Genius in You

That's the kind of self-confidence and charisma that I want you to reclaim.

We all have it when we are children.

Reading this book, you have a challenge: you're very intelligent.

When we grow up, our parents, society, the media, and the schools tell us that we should use our intellect primarily to do one thing: to doubt ourselves! We are told that we should make comparisons between ourselves and others, not to find out where we are strong, but to concentrate on our lacks, weaknesses, flaws, and mistakes.

This is not the intellect's primary natural purpose. Nor is it its tendency or function.

A lack of natural self-confidence is an acquired and learned cultural phenomenon, something that you can unlearn and change.

We just have to remind ourselves of that and forget about all the mental clutter that is thrown our way when we grow up.

Transform Your Inner Critic into Your Best Success Coach

Transforming your inner critic into your best success coach is simple. Think back to the previous episode.

We all have that success coach within us. We are born with it.

You are your own greatest and most effective coach and motivator. You just have to rediscover that inner success coach that you've had all along. Use that fantastic intellect of yours to remember your past successes, large or small.

Do this every day for five minutes.

All the successful people I know dwell on their successes, focus on them, exhibit them, remember them, cherish them, and rejoice in them.

They make a ritual out of this. They decorate their homes with their successes. They hang up pictures and images showing them at their peak moments in life.

To get you back into your superconfidence mode, I want you to start telling yourself how well you're doing as you go about your day. Use your intellect to find even the smallest things you're good at!

Success builds success. Our biggest successes are built on the shoulders of our smaller ones.

Before going to bed at night, I reflect on the biggest success of my day. I also remember the happiest moments and the times when I was most in the "zone," that wonderful state of free flow when we are at our creative and personal best. The whole routine takes no more than a minute.

Anything you remember right before dozing off to sleep will have an even more powerful effect than if you remembered it during the day. You literally take this with you into the dream state, thereby setting yourself up for even more and bigger successes the next day.

Use Anchors and Triggers

When Mick Jagger goes on stage, he turns into a creative lunatic with a massive amount of power and energy. The stage is his turbocharger.

But I was astounded by what a cool, calm, and decent English gentleman he is when you talk to him offstage. I thought to myself: "This cannot possibly be the same guy!"

It's the stage that does it for him. It's his personal trigger and anchor that helps him transform himself into that bigger Mick, the legendary rock star—that crazy guy who hops around like an 18-year-old for two hours and makes three generations of fans go wild. And this at an age when most people are checking into a retirement home.

A friend of mine is the founder and owner of a very successful multinational software company. He always wears a ring that he bought after his biggest professional breakthrough success. The ring constantly reminds him of his biggest successes.

While Gary has since acquired many wonderful possessions, including several yachts and properties around the world, this ring is still his most prized possession.

Why? He says it embodies and symbolizes his capacity to create whatever success he wants and to accomplish whatever he puts his mind to.

You can do the same. Use something that you can see often during your day. A ring, watch, bracelet, or something else that you can wear on your hands is ideal. It could also be a piece of clothing—whatever works.

Maximum visibility is the key. And it has to have a very strong personal meaning for you.

Make it a trigger to remind you of your greatest success.

Meet Your Future Self—the Person You Want to Become

For his leading role in the movie *The Last Tycoon*, Robert De Niro had to portray a Hollywood studio tycoon at the beginning of the twentieth century. In preparation for his role, De Niro walked through the grounds of the big Hollywood studios every day for weeks, repeating the same phrase to himself over and over again: "All of this is mine. All of this is mine."

Learn from actors like Robert De Niro and musicians like Mick Jagger. Anything can be your stage.

Use verbal commands and the props you have available—from a stage to a boardroom—to help you grow into that bigger version of yourself. Have fun and play! Act!

All the great businessmen, entrepreneurs, artists, and top achievers in any field are actors because they turn every day and every important milestone in their career or business into a meeting with their future self, the person they want to grow into and become.

They tune in to that bigger version of themselves.

Whether it's Mick Jagger going on stage or you going for your next job interview, starting your own company, or going into your next board meeting, it's always the same process.

Tune in to the person you want to become. Play! Act! Have fun with it!

Follow Your Role Models

Kids play with role models all the time. They pretend they are doctors, parents, teachers, or whatever role they want to try out. This is how they grow.

When children do this, we think it's natural. When adults do it, we think it's stupid.

But it's one of the most powerful tools we have available.

One of the biggest obstacles that you may face is the limiting belief that you think you cannot teach or train yourself to become self-confident—you either have it or you don't. That's complete nonsense.

While I was superconfident as a child, I lost it somewhere along the way and became terribly shy and timid. Overcoming shyness and becoming self-confident is a skill that can be learned, just like any other.

Copy your role models.

Imagine that you already are the person you want to become. Tell yourself that you are the best, the biggest, the greatest, the number one in the world! Or that you're the next . . . (whatever role model you admire most).

Superstar Rihanna certainly did that. When she was growing up, she always told herself that she was going to become the next Madonna. She skyrocketed to success in an unbelievably short period of time.

And guess what role model Madonna chose in achieving her superstardom? Michael Jackson.

She revealed in an interview that Michael was her biggest idol when she was growing up. By tuning in to Michael Jackson and the way he had become a legend and an icon in the music industry, Madonna transferred the same qualities to herself, her own life, and her career in music. So she became an icon herself.

EXERCISE: Catapult Yourself to Superconfidence Again!

Time needed: 1 minute

Look at the different tools, tips, tricks, triggers, anchors, and best practices I have shared in this chapter, and pick the one that you think works best for you.

Take that item and decide to implement it *now*.

You can still change it along the way, modify and adapt it, or switch to another one. But the most important thing is that you put one of these ideas into practice now.

This will make sure you get into the groove of taking action. Awaken the confident child within! You're a genius!

See you at the puzzle.

Confidence is contagious. So is lack of confidence.
—Vince Lombardi

All you need is ignorance and confidence and the success is sure.
—Mark Twain

Points to Remember

We are all born self-confident. Often we lose our self-confidence as we grow up because we are taught to compare ourselves with others to see where we come up short. We learn to focus on our flaws and weaknesses instead of on our talents, strengths, and successes.

Self-confidence and charisma can be relearned and reacquired easily.

You are your own greatest and most effective success coach and motivator.

Learn from the tips, tricks, and best practices of successful artists, actors, and entrepreneurs to create your biggest successes in your personal life, career, or business.

Success builds success. Our biggest successes are built on the shoulders of our smaller ones.

Step 4

Harness Your Creative Power

A Poem a Day Keeps Foreclosure Away: How Creativity Can Help You Unleash Your True Power

> We [at Sony] are always chasing after things that other companies won't touch. That is a big secret to our success.
> —Norio Ohga, former chairman of Sony

The Painting That Saved My Business

I had just awakened after 12 hours of sleep. My body was a wreck. I had no energy. I was completely overworked and out of balance. My biggest project at the time, the World Peace Festival and the World Peace Foundation, was at an important crossroads. It was either going to go belly up or reach a major breakthrough success.

I needed help and answers. And I needed them fast.

I told my wife to pack. I booked a hotel room in Marseille for the weekend, which was an hour and a half away from where we lived. While we were packing, I suddenly had an impulse to paint. I was a prolific singer, songwriter, and pianist but I had never painted before—at least, not since I was a child.

I went out and bought canvases, paint, and brushes. It was a weird feeling. Whenever we try something new and conquer uncharted territory, it takes courage.

Late that night, once we were settled in and my wife was fast asleep, I took a leap of faith and entered a new world. Brush in hand, I slowly started to put paint on canvas.

Art and Your Inner Guidance System

I still have the painting I created that night. It had a meaning that touched me on a deep level. When I look at it today, it still captures the whirlwind that I was in and that it showed me the way out of at the same time. It allowed my intuition to come to the fore in a situation where I needed it most. In hindsight, picking up painting at that time in my life enabled me to tap into my inner guidance system and allowed me to find the greater solutions that I needed. I was able to get back on course.

On the drive home, I felt rebalanced already. I called my assistant and my team, and I took the first steps necessary for a course correction. Painting allowed me to look at everything from a larger perspective.

It saved my business.

The Soul Speaks Through Art

I have since learned that the important course corrections and insights that are vital for my successes in business and the major decisions in my life show themselves first in my art, whether it's through writing, poetry, music, or even painting, as in the story above.

All creative artists have an outlet, a medium of expression, whether it's music, poetry, painting, photography, writing, sculpting, acting—you name it.

The soul speaks through art. Being creative is a way to be in touch with your own inner guidance system. This allows you to have a better connection with your inner senses and your inner voice.

Art serves as a way to express those intuitions and impulses that otherwise might not be heard at all or might come to the fore only much later.

As a result of art, your decisions are much better; you have what I call "the internal buy-in" to set the right goals that actually work for you (see the section "Set Goals That Really Work") and the intuitions about what steps to take to achieve them. As a result, your performance and your success will soar!

Your Inner Search Engine for the World Wide Web

Have you ever wondered why you just knew something before it happened? Why you became scared at the sound of a car accident before you actually heard the tires screeching?

We all have access to a powerhouse of infinite information. We are connected to everything in the universe, as if a giant web unites us all.

The World Wide Web is a good analogy. Imagine that you have a built-in search function for the universe—one that has no limits on what information you can obtain and provides search results instantaneously. This would be a dream come true for my friends at Google!

Ways of creative expression, in whatever form, allow you to sharpen your inner senses and improve your inner search engine.

This is not limited to information from the inside (the important decisions you have to take, the goals you set for yourself, and so on), but also includes information from the outside. You might have an intuition that a supplier will go out of business before he does. You might have a hunch that you shouldn't do business with a certain person, even though that person comes highly recommended and her CV looks awesome (trust me, this has happened to me countless times!). You might resist signing a contract even though, on the surface, it looks perfect.

Calligraphy and the Birth of the First Mac

As Steve Jobs said in his famous Stanford commencement address in 2005: "You can't connect the dots looking forward." What he meant was that your intellect can't, but your gut and your intuition can. This is why he went on to say: "Because believing that the dots will connect down the road will give you the confidence to follow your heart, even when it leads you off the well-worn path."

This is why the game-changing CEOs and legendary high achievers in any field, the people who outperform and leave us all in awe, have found their own creative ways to express themselves.

After dropping out of college, Steve Jobs followed an urge to study calligraphy and went on to single-mindedly immerse himself in his calligraphy studies for 18 months. He later credited this with being instrumental in designing the key features of the Mac: "When we were designing the first Macintosh computer, it all came back to me. And we designed it all into the Mac. It was the first computer with beautiful typography. If I had never dropped in on that single course in college, the Mac would have never had multiple typefaces or proportionally spaced fonts."

The CEO Who Conducted Symphonies and Invented the CD

Norio Ohga was the former president and chairman of Sony. Not only was he the youngest president in the history of Sony, but he was also credited with having developed the CD.

Norio was a CEO who understood the benefits of a whole, eclectic approach to business. He was able to invent the CD only because he was an accomplished baritone singer and symphonic conductor. In fact, he was so proficient in music that he was asked to conduct two symphonies at the prestigious Schleswig-Holstein Music Festival in Germany, where his name appeared alongside those of other eminent conductors.

He had a tech mind and a creative mind, and he learned how to combine the two to come up with new levels of solutions that no one else could see.

Think Both, Not Either/Or

In his inspirational book, *Secrets of the Millionaire Mind*, T. Harv Eker explains that successful and fulfilled people think in terms of "both," while most unsuccessful people think in terms of "either/or."

Here is how Norio Ohga prepared for his performance. With only months to learn two symphonies, Ohga devoted three hours a night to his scores. About 2 o'clock each morning, he rose and headed for his study. He returned to bed at 5 and was awakened two hours later by a call from Sony's U.S. chief, whose business day was just ending. Talk about applying the concept of *both* big time!

Now, for you, you don't need to be conducting a symphony orchestra. You can just be in your living room. It's not about the quality of your work. The point is not to reach excellence or even to be any good.

Give yourself permission to *suck*!

The key is to express yourself creatively in whatever way possible, even if it's just a personal journal you keep in which you make an entry every day.

EXERCISE: Your Creative Power
Total time required: 3 minutes

Step 1: Brainstorm
Time required: 2 minutes

Take two minutes to make a list of creative activities you have always wanted to try but never did, or things that you tried at some point and enjoyed but have not done for a long time. These could include keeping a journal, writing a blog, writing a poem, playing the guitar, dancing, drawing, painting, sculpting, acting—you name it.

If you are doing something creative already, either in your job or as a hobby, but you feel stuck, try something different. Think about what other creative activities you could try that would be fun. For me, in the earlier anecdote, that was painting.

Don't Let Limiting Beliefs Hold You Back
Some mental blocks might get in your way:
1. "What if I'm not creative?" We all are. *You* are. You just have to find what works for *you*—there are countless ways to express your creativity.
2. "What if I don't have time?" You might think that doing something creative is a waste of time, a detour from your work and your goals.

Trust me: it will actually *save* you time. You will know *what* to do, *how* to do it, and *when* to do it, and you will do it much *faster*. This will lead to better performance, happiness, and success in all areas of your life.

You might find other excuses ("have to work," "have no money," and so on). All these excuses will actually be your resistance to change. Remember the chapter that talks about how to reach your goals: "Embrace Change"! Go for it! Give it a shot!

Step 2: Let's Do It!
Time required: 1 minute

Once you have completed your list, take another minute to look at it and decide *now* which activity you will try. Again, you are not going for Carnegie Hall, so quality doesn't matter.

Get in front of the mirror and say: "I hereby grant you the license to *suck*!"

Your only goal is to find a way to express yourself creatively so that you can make better decisions in business and the other areas of your life, which will ultimately lead to much better performance, greater happiness, and more success!

You know my philosophy: start small.

Ask yourself, what is the single next action I can take to move this forward?

Schedule this action in your diary *now*. If you have to go out and buy paint, schedule it. If you have to make your first journal entry, schedule it. If you have to dust off that old guitar, schedule it. You want to take singing lessons? Schedule it.

Videos: Steve Jobs's Stanford Commencement Address

This is a classic. If you haven't seen it already, I strongly urge you to make it a high priority on your YouTube bookmarks. The part about calligraphy and its impact on the birth of the first Mac comes at 4:00 minutes.

In YouTube, type "Steve Jobs' 2005 Stanford Commencement Address."

(This is the official version from Stanford University.)

> ### Points to Remember
>
> If you have a way to express yourself creatively, it will put you in a frame of mind where you can make much better decisions in business and in life.
>
> You will know what to do, how to do it, and when to do it, and you will do it much faster. This will lead to better performance, greater happiness, and more success in all areas of your life.

How to Kill Perfectionism and Get Everything Done You've Ever Dreamed Of—and More!

> Perfectionism is the voice of the oppressor.
> —Anne Lamott

> The fastest way to break the cycle of perfectionism and become a fearless mother is to give up the idea of doing it perfectly—indeed to embrace uncertainty and imperfection.
> —Arianna Huffington

It was 2 a.m.

I had always been a perfectionist, but now it was driving me crazy.

Here I was, 16 years old, used to being an A student back in Germany, but now sitting in history class with the best students in the United States. English was my third language, and there was no way I could complete the hundreds of pages of reading assignments every day, let alone get good grades!

I was on a scholarship at one of the best boarding schools in the world, Choate Rosemary Hall in Connecticut, pulling another one of my famous all-nighters.

I was struggling, to say the least. Exhausted and on the verge of utter despair, I was doing six hours of homework a day and more.

Then my history teacher took me aside and taught me one of the most important lessons of my life: "Tom, it doesn't have to be perfect the first time you go over *any* material. Instead, you go over it many times and fill in the gaps."

Wow.

As in all great breakthrough moments, those true epiphanies, you know when you have hit something big. And I had just been given the key to getting rid of perfectionism.

A year later, I was standing on a podium in the hot summer sun, holding my diploma in my hand. I was the first foreign student in the history of the school to come in at the fifth form (eleventh grade) level, skip a class, and graduate in the same year.

The key not only to taking in information, but also to creating *anything* in your life and reaching your optimum potential, is to go over the same thing many times and fill in the gaps.

It absolutely doesn't matter how well you do something the first time or any other time you go over it.

This will free up your energy and put you into superachiever mode.

The Modern Way to Make a Record

Fast-forward to many years later.

I was lying on the cold bathroom floor. I had just regained consciousness and started to throw up.

It didn't take a genius to know that I had clearly overdone it this time.

I was in the middle of recording my new songs at one of Europe's biggest studios. And I was wondering why I felt so miserable when I was actually doing what I loved.

Why did the rehearsal with the band give me so much energy, but the actual recording in the studio drained the hell out of me?

Then I realized: I had succumbed to the industry's perverse standards of perfection, and it had sucked the life out of both me and the recording.

You see, in the old days, when the Rolling Stones and the Beatles were new, there wasn't the kind of sophisticated computer recording equipment that we have today. Most of the recordings were done in a few takes, and all of them had to be done more or less live.

Nowadays you have what is called the "sandwich" technique: You record endless takes, sometimes up to several hundred, and then you slice them up into little pieces. In the end, the "I" in "I love you" is from take 85, the "love" is from take 97, and the "you" is from take 205. There are infinite layers of recording after recording in a sandwich technique, one musician after another, never playing together.

On top of this, everything has to be synced to the computer's internal clock. This means no improvisation on tempo changes; everything has to be timed to perfection. Imagine a robot hitting his head on a door while being strapped to a pacemaker.

Insanity!

Live or Not Live? That Is the Question

This insanity rules even in jazz, the all-time haven of improvisation and spontaneity.

One of my band members told me about his meeting with a famous jazz musician, Wynton Marsalis.

Wynton said to him: "We are just mixing my new album. You want to come over and have a listen?"

"Sure!" Felix said.

They went over into the mixing room, and Wynton played him his songs.

"Let's listen to this new song I made. This is from take 31. And this piece here is from take 89. And this one is from take 185."

You get the idea.

If you think classical music is an exception, you are mistaken. Classical studio recordings are cut to death—even worse than any other genre. Not even a few seconds that you hear on any classical recording today were ever played like that in real time.

The same goes for albums labeled "live." Without embarrassing anyone, I know famous singers who go back into the studio to record over their "live" albums to make them bearable.

There were rumors that Madonna fired one of her producers because he went on TV and said that she couldn't sing, so he had to pump her voice through nine different machines to make it sound the way it does. That was no news to the music industry.

For years, musicians have gotten a laugh out of the bootleg recording of Enrique Iglesias's voice that a sound engineer took during one of his live concerts, because it was so bad.

Get over it, guys—welcome to the music business.

Everything Is a Rehearsal

> Have no fear of perfection. You'll never reach it.
> —Salvador Dalì

> Perfectionism is not a quest for the best. It is a pursuit of the worst in ourselves,
> the part that tells us that nothing we do will ever be good enough.
> —Julia Cameron, *The Artist's Way*

I'm in a big stadium, and the Rolling Stones are on tour. It's raining heavily, and Keith Richards is puffing on a cigarette. He's having the time of his life putting on a crazy guitar riff.

The guys are having fun, and it shows! Yes, they make mistakes, because they are playing live. But that's why they are one of the greatest rock bands of all time, in operation for 50 years.

It's good to have high standards, but not when they're so high that you are actually limiting your ability to get things done.

I had a dream once in which a voice told me: "Tom, when you adopt the attitude that everything is a rehearsal, you will do so much better!"

And it's true. Your energy and performance at anything will be a lot better—more natural and more spontaneous—and you will succeed with ease.

I was standing on Kite Beach in Maui talking to a friend of mine, Mike Eskimo. Mike is a legend who has been known to push the boundaries of traditional surfing, whether it is to ride giant waves with his hands in handcuffs, to surf over hot lava gushing into the Pacific, or to be the first to do three-meter aerials on a stand-up paddle board.

"You know, many of those guys from around the world come here and want to look good. We are trying new things all the time, and when you do that, you look bad. That's how you become a pro."

Give yourself permission to look bad—and screw up!

The more you are willing to look bad while you are still in the stages of going over something again and again, the better you will be—and look—in the end.

If you are suffering from perfectionism, try to adopt the attitude of a live concert: life is a rehearsal—*all* the time. Then your productivity will soar because your perfectionism will no longer block you from living your energy and actually doing the work. Only doing the work will make you any better.

Once you free yourself up to make mistakes, you will instantly improve and will have much more fun doing it.

Getting rid of perfectionism is, ironically, the fastest way to get close to being "perfect"—in any sense of the word.

The Smallest Step

Here's how I wrote this book.

I used a simple technique to get over my perfectionist tendencies.

I started with the smallest possible step: I put my ideas on index cards. They are not intimidating, and it seemed doable. I was excited at how fast I could fill them up with ideas. I even used a pencil and not a pen to give myself the feeling that what I wrote wasn't carved in stone, and I could still change whatever I wanted when I went over it.

Then I put everything on paper in longhand or directly into my MacBook.

Then I printed out each chapter and made the necessary edits on paper.

Then I changed the text on my laptop and printed it out again.

I repeated this cycle as many times as necessary until I was done. It's simple!

The key, again, is to go over it many times, making changes and editing, so that the next step always seems small and doable, and I never fall into the trap of thinking it has to be perfect.

As my history teacher said, go over it many times and fill in the gaps. And I would add: start with the smallest step.

Everything is a rehearsal!

Just as there are a million ways to write a song, there are endless alternative versions of the same end result, and guess what? They are all good!

So just pick one and run with it.

This works equally well when you are facing a pressing deadline, have to submit a last-minute paper, or have to finish an important project that's due in an hour! The same principle applies to crises or even life-threatening situations or dilemmas.

You always take the smallest possible step, readdress it, and go over it again and again until you end up with the result you need.

Done!

EXERCISE: Music to Your Ears

Time needed: exactly 10:24 minutes

This is a listening exercise.

"Now that You Know" by Carlos Santana (recorded live on his tour in 1985) is from the album *Blues for Salvador*.

Carlos is one of the all-time masters when it comes to live performances. He doesn't care about keeping in line with the tempo of the song. He just rocks and goes with the energy.

This is why his live performances and recordings are jam-packed with enormous energy that makes most hits on today's charts look lifeless.

When you listen to that song, a 10:24-minute tour de force of Carlos rocking his brains out, you can hear tempo changes where he and the band are improvising the hell out of it. Even if you have absolutely no ear for music or tempo changes and couldn't care less, you can hear that the song has different energies throughout. Carlos changes the tempo again and again to go *with* the energy of the song. The tempo follows the song, not the other way around.

By the way, the album won the 1989 Grammy Award for Best Rock Instrumental Performance. You will know why!

EXERCISE: Do It! Now!

Time needed: 5 minutes

Take something you have been putting off for a while because your demands on yourself or for the end result were so high that you were getting in your own way. Then ask yourself: what would be the *smallest* next step to take this toward completion?

Write it down.

Then *do it! Now!*

When you catch yourself in that perfectionist mood again and get stuck, tell yourself: "Quality literally doesn't matter. I will go over it again and again until it's done."

Quality comes from not getting in your own way and just letting it flow, not from your own crazy ideas about what the perfect first draft should look like.

Everybody's first drafts suck. Big time.

Release the brakes and enjoy the ride!

> Nothing that is complete breathes.
> —Antonio Porchia, Argentinean poet

> Perfectionism becomes a badge of honor with you
> playing the part of the suffering hero.
> —David D. Burns, adjunct professor emeritus,
> Stanford University School of Medicine

Points to Remember

It's good to have high standards, but not when they're so high that you are actually limiting your ability to get things done.

If you are suffering from perfectionism, try to adopt the attitude that life is a rehearsal—all the time. Once you free yourself up to make mistakes, you will instantly improve and will have much more fun doing it. Then your productivity will soar because your perfectionism will no longer block you from living your energy and actually doing the work. Only doing the work will make you any better.

The key to taking in information, creating anything in your life, and reaching your optimum potential is to start with the smallest step. Then you go over the same thing again and again and fill in the gaps. It absolutely doesn't matter how well you do something the first time or any other time you go over it.

This will free up your energy and put you into superachiever mode.

The Zone: A State of Peak Performance Where Your Best Work Happens with Ease

Simplicity is the key to brilliance.
—Bruce Lee

Mille viae ducunt homines per saecula Romam.
(A thousand roads will always lead to Rome.)
—Roman proverb

I was snowboarding down a mountain in the Swiss Alps, surrounded by white bliss.

Suddenly something clicked, and I got into the zone. Everything fell into place; mind and body became *one*. I just had to think of a move, and there it was—executed beautifully. Wherever I looked, there I went, jumping high into the air.

I felt one with my mind, my body, the mountains, the beautiful scenery, the trees, and the people around me. It was a state of peak performance in which everything seemed effortless.

To this day, this is still one of the best snowboard rides I have ever had, an experience that has ingrained itself into my cellular memory. The "zone" is a peak performance state where your best work happens with ease. Some athletes have called it "the flow," surfers call it "the ride," and creative artists call it "jamming," among many other terms.

It's a state in which you are pushing your boundaries with ease and living your true potential. The good news is: this can be applied to any area or activity in your life.

The Zone Takes Care of Quality Automatically, Without Our Intellect Getting in the Way

In the section "Flip It!," I talk about how I was a serious stutterer as a child and how I cured it. Besides the fact that I had to learn to trust myself and my own energy, there was still another mental side to it. Stutterers are usually perfectionists. We set the bar too high and do not let communication flow. This perfectionism causes us to stutter.

The process can be equally applied to action and performance in any area. There is no single perfect way to do anything well. We have to trust that we will express ourselves or accomplish whatever we are setting out to do. Then we have to let ourselves go and ride our own energy while keeping our eyes firmly fixed on the outcome, the conceptualized mental image of our ideal; the flow of our impulses will then take care of the rest. Once you let yourself fall and get into the zone, your best work will happen with ease, and it will not feel like "work" at all.

This is key. You have to trust your own energy and let yourself go.

Get your damned head out of the way! This is a challenge for intellectually gifted people. I see this again and again, both in my students at business school and in real life with people with high potential in any area, from the creative arts to business. A high IQ means that you tend to use your intellect as a stop sign. In fact, we have been taught to use our intellect as a stop sign, to overanalyze and not trust ourselves. We want to be *perfect*. There are literally a million roads you can take to accomplish, do, or say anything and achieve great results. Perfectionism assumes that there is only one single best way to do something. We wrack our brains to find that one best way and to live up to that standard. This mindset is often the fastest road to misery and mediocrity, as we are cutting ourselves off from our own energy source and fall short of ever reaching our full potential, what we're truly capable of.

It's important to realize that this behavior is simply a culturally acquired habit, not something innate. You can get rid of it easily. In fact, *all* great entrepreneurs, businesspeople, CEOs, artists, athletes, and peak performers in any area have done so. They know that all they have to do is to get into the zone, and it will take care of quality automatically. Remember that the next time you're under pressure to perform well. Your intellect is a tool. The zone is the master.

The Concert

The other day, I was performing live with my band in the South of France. In the days before the concert, my head had been filled with clutter and debris, the kind of mental worries that we lose ourselves in way too often.

When it came to performing, I wasn't in the moment at all. I was winding my mental tape forward or backward a few minutes, hours, or days. I wasn't *here now*.

We started our performance, and the music helped me to slowly let myself go, get into the zone, and ride my energy. I became one with the other band members, one with the rhythm, one with the movement of my hands touching the piano, one with the beat, and one with the DJ spinning the sounds.

And suddenly the party exploded! Boom! I could feel the waves of energy touching the whole band and then the audience. I looked at Nicolas, who was feverishly hitting the drums, then at my sax player, Felix, and we all had big grins on our faces. It was so much fun! Later, one of my band members came to me and said: "You put your fire into it!" It was his way of saying: "You let yourself go!"

Anyone can achieve a state like that by letting himself go and letting his own natural energy shine. We make things way too difficult. Concentrate on the outcome; take away the mental barriers, obstacles, and old stop signs. Ride that wave of your own inner energy into the zone, and you will be in a peak performance state in no time.

Dropping In: Jamming

> Music can change the world because it can change people.
> —Bono

> It's only by jamming that you can get a song together.
> —Maurice Gibb

In music, the zone happens when you are at your creative best and you let your juices flow, both when you are playing alone and when you are playing with a band. In jamming, the best creative ideas come to life, and that's clearly when the best recordings are made. A lot of great live performances can never be translated one to one into a studio recording because in the studio, things are engineered to perfection until you receive a polished image of something that is a poor reproduction of what happens on stage. When you've got a great band and you have a oneness in that band, you naturally get into the zone. You jam. This is how great music is made.

Some of the best recordings were made when bands like Carlos Santana or the Rolling Stones recorded a lot of their songs live, without cutting the hell out of them. If you won't take my word for it, take any chart topper of today, then listen to Carlos Santana rocking his brains out on "Now That You Know" from the *Blues for Salvador* album. You will know what I mean. You don't even have to like Carlos's music.

No Strain Is Required

The zone is a state in which your skills are trained at an optimum level and you are actually pushing the boundaries of your own potential with ease. No strain is required. All you have to do is let yourself go. Some of my most productive creative writing sessions used to happen on planes because I felt mentally disconnected from the rest of the world. The pressures of daily life were lifted. The lyrics to one of my most successful songs, "Free Your Mind," were written high up between the clouds. Now I know I don't have to get on a plane to achieve that state; I can produce it anywhere, any time—and so can you!

Be playful about it and use the zone to unlock your hidden potentials in any area. Enjoy the ride. The good news is: you will have loads of fun doing it!

Dropping In: My First Time on a Snowboard

The hardest part is overcoming the fear of directing the board into the fall line of the slope. You're up on that gnarly mountain. You are freezing your tail off. Your knees are killing you. But you gotta get down. You finally turn the board into the fall line—and trust. Your stomach contracts; you're gaining speed rapidly. You wonder whether you will first crash into the trees to your left or do a double flip on the icy patch ahead and land face down with a dislocated jaw.

Then the magic happens. You start to look where you want to go. Your head turns, your shoulders turn with it, and suddenly the board turns with them, taking you exactly where you want to go. Before you know it, you're gliding effortlessly down the slopes, mastering every turn by changing the direction and focus of your eyes. Your body and the board do the rest.

The mountain, ice, snow, people, trees, and everything else become secondary in that fluid magic carpet ride. You feel as if you are traveling back in time to the days when you were a little kid gliding down a water slide and giggling with joy. And your smile was so wide that it had to be surgically removed.

All surfers and boarders who have that grin on their face know that surfing is a great parallel for life. Some great lessons can be transferred from surfing to other areas of our life to allow us to produce masterpieces with ease and in complete harmony with nature and the pulsating rhythms of our own energy. Look where you want to go, release all controls, let yourself fall into the zone, and trust that life will take care of the rest.

Have fun while performing at your peak!

Tool: Use Suggestions

A great way to get yourself into the zone is to use verbal suggestions. They act like short mantras that provide a hypnotic focus. Repeating the same verbal suggestion to yourself over and over again is a fantastic tool to help you get into a state of free flow. You will have to try it out a bit until you find the suggestion that works best for you, depending on the circumstances and on the goal you want to accomplish.

I personally find short suggestions to be most effective. But we are all unique. Trust your own inner guidance system and work with different suggestions to see which ones produce the best results and get you into the zone fastest.

Whatever verbal suggestion you choose, repeat it to yourself over and over again, and at some point you will naturally get into that state of free flow. Surfing is a good analogy: You ride that wave of your own energy; you trust and go with it, and the wave will take care of the rest.

Not For the Faint of Heart: Extremes

A trick is to put yourself into a very challenging or even extreme life situation. You will find that the extreme pressure will force you to mentally hypnotize yourself out of it in no time. I have certainly done this many times over, from nearly drowning to kitesurfing 15-foot waves to setting myself almost insurmountable physical, mental, business, and life challenges. While this certainly works for me, instantly pushing my boundaries and letting me discover the right suggestions in no time, it is not for everyone. I'm hyperactive, I'm a thrill seeker, and I tend to go to extremes because boredom is my enemy. If it does not fit your lifestyle, there's no need to go to extremes.

EXERCISE: Remember the Zone

Time needed: 5 minutes

For one week, I want you to take five minutes a day to remember past successes and moments when you felt fully immersed in the zone. Close your eyes and think back to times when you were at your creative best, when you achieved true personal mastery and did so with ease because you let yourself go. You might not have called it the zone, you might not even have realized that a state like that existed, but the results were still obvious. The simple act of searching your past for such states will reveal them to you. Then try to replay these instances in your mind. Images or sounds might appear. Allow yourself to indulge in those sensations for a while.

The simple act of remembering these peak performance states will reactivate your cellular memory and serve as a trigger to create similar experiences in your life. This exercise may even lead to a state in which you get into the zone without being consciously aware of it, and you realize only afterward what actually happened. This is great because it means that you truly let yourself go.

In case you have never experienced a state like this before, use some of the examples I've given here, from surfing to music. See how you could apply these to the areas in your life where you want to be at your creative and productive best. Then create an imaginary situation in your mind where you approach a peak performance state with ease and ride that wave of your own energy.

Trust me. After you do this exercise, the zone will show up in your life in no time, and you, too, will become a peak performer. Unleash the rock star in you!

Option: Re-create the Ideal Conditions

Time needed: 3 minutes

Ask yourself: what were the conditions that led to those experiences, those states of joy and mastery where you pushed your boundaries with ease? Try to find some underlying conditions or common routines that unite all of these experiences. Once you start looking for them, they will become obvious.

Block out times in your diary for a meeting with yourself and the zone. Then consciously try to re-create those conditions and routines in your daily life.

EXERCISE: Check In Before Falling Asleep

Time needed: 30 seconds

Every night before I fall asleep, I ask myself: when was I most in the zone today? If nothing comes to my mind on that particular day, I go back to the days before. I try to relive those moments of peak performance, the state of joy that comes with them, and the immense ease and effortlessness that accompany our best and most productive states. A lot of the time, 30 seconds is all it takes. On other days, I may have to do this for a minute or two. In any case, just the simple act of remembering the zone is enough to trigger similar future experiences. You will then take this experience and realization into the dream state and set yourself up for even bigger successes the next day.

Suggestion is no more and no less than an inner
willingness and consent to allow a particular action to occur;
and this consent is the trigger which sets off the subconscious
mechanisms that allow you to construct inner data into physical reality.
—Jane Roberts, *The Seth Material*

Points to Remember

The zone is a state of peak performance where your skills are trained at an optimum level and you are pushing the boundaries of your own potential with ease. All you have to do is let yourself go and recognize the conditions that lead to such states.

Then ride your own energy, look where you want to go, and keep your eyes firmly fixed on the outcome (the conceptualized mental image of your goal). The flow of your impulses will take care of the rest. Once you let yourself fall and get into that zone, your best work will happen with ease, and it will not feel like "work" at all.

You can use the zone to unlock your hidden potentials and reach a peak performance state in *any* area. You can induce such a state anywhere, any time, in whatever area of your life for whatever results you want to accomplish. And the good news is: you will have loads of fun doing it!

The Invisible Hands: The Secret Behind the Creative Process

The creative process is a process of surrender, not control.
—Julia Cameron, *The Artist's Way*

I write the book that wants to be written. Behind the first sentence is a thread that takes you to the last.
—Paulo Coelho

I was sitting next to the writer Paulo Coelho, who wrote the inspirational worldwide bestseller *The Alchemist* and whose books have sold more than 100 million copies. We were at the Cannes Film Festival, and it was Naomi Campbell's birthday party.

"The book is the boss," Paulo said. "You have to trust the creative process and just let it flow."

"The book is the boss," he repeated. I nodded and smiled. Paulo meant that you may have a certain concept in mind as to what your book is all about. You may even have taken notes on paper and put some initial ideas down. But once you sit down to actually write the book, the creative process takes over, and you are no longer in control.

You have to step back and let the magic happen.

This applies equally to anything you are setting out to create, whether it is starting your own business, creating a new product or service, or bringing a new project to life.

You may believe that your initial ideas are the best in the world, you may even have an exact plan for how you want to go about it, but in the end, the book is the boss. This means that every creative project or idea has its own energy, and you had better go with that energy and surrender yourself to it.

You have to follow and trust that process. This is the key to getting fantastic results.

You Need a Minimum Structure

Hendrik was the star of the party. We were 16, and he was a gifted young piano player who could bring any house down. I couldn't get very far with my Rachmaninoff and Chopin. Somehow the classics weren't nearly as exciting as what Hendrik was doing.

One evening I took him aside and asked: "How do you manage to play like that? What's the secret?"

He showed me a pop music sheet with chords on it. He explained what the chords meant and how to play them. I sat down, looked at the chords, and tried it.

"But that doesn't sound like you!" I said, disappointed.

He laughed: "Of course, you don't just put the chords down. That sounds boring. The chords provide the basics, the foundation. Then you put feeling into it and improvise, always taking the chords as a foundation. You simply play around the chords."

I smiled. "Click."

I learned that in every business, team setting, project, idea, product, or service that you want to bring to life, you need a minimum structure that sets the stage for the creative process to unfold.

Once the necessary structure is set, though, you have to step back and let the magic happen.

Let the Magic Happen: The Secret
Behind Creativity and Innovation

Just as in music, there's a fine line. You need just enough structure to enable the creative process to happen, to give it room. But if you are too focused on structure, you will stifle the creative process and suck the life and soul out of it.

This is why great innovation happens only when businesses or individuals understand the creative process. And it's not linear. As my friend Jez Frampton, the global CEO of Interbrand and the number one authority on branding in the world, likes to say: "Businesses don't jam enough." He's right.

Creativity and innovation are the two biggest drivers of long-term success for any business, corporate brand, or multinational. For the last five years, corporations have been focusing on cutting costs out of the supply side. Now small businesses and big multinationals alike have to focus on building the demand side, and here innovation is the biggest issue. Now more than ever, the ability of any business to consistently produce innovation at the highest level determines its long-term success. Since the innovation process is not linear, businesses and big corporations can profit immensely from understanding the creative process better and how it can be used to produce optimum results in innovation.

You have to trust this process. This means that you have to *step back* and *let the magic happen*.

In music, structure might mean setting up the studio, taking care of the band, and the basics of the recording. For example, everybody has to have copies of the music to give them a basic idea of where we are going. But then the flow, the "jamming," will take care of the rest. The magic happens once you step back and let the energy flow.

If you're running a business or a project, do your best to provide the minimum framework that is necessary to let the creative process unfold. However, you cannot turn into a control freak. If you do, the creative process is dead.

Your project, idea, service, or product will have a life and energy of its own, and you have to trust and go with that energy. It will have better sense than you.

The "One": Focus on What You Want to Express or Create

> Don't try to innovate storytelling, tell a good story and it is magical.
> I see people trying to work so much in style, finding different ways
> to tell the same thing. It's like fashion. Style is the dress,
> but the dress does not dictate what is inside the dress.
> —Paulo Coelho

> I don't know exactly where ideas come from, but when I'm working
> well ideas just appear. I've heard other people say similar things—
> so it's one of the ways I know there's help and guidance
> out there. It's just a matter of our figuring out how to receive the
> ideas or information that are waiting to be heard.
> —Jim Henson

When I'm writing a new song or playing with the band, I always focus on one central image, the meaning of the song that I want to get across. That central image, the "one," as I call it, serves as the basis for everything I'm doing when I'm in the zone and playing.

Equally, there is a one that guides the creative process behind every project, product, service, or business.

You have to focus on it to make whatever you are doing truly outstanding. In musical composition, this one will evolve naturally. I start with the chords or the lyrics, and then the one will emerge if I give myself up to the song.

Every business fulfills, or should fulfill, a need, and it is precisely that need that is at the core of every corporate vision. When it comes to business, the one central theme, motto, vision, or mission that your company is built on, just like Bill Gates's motto "A PC in every home," will be your focus and your guide. Once you fully concentrate on the one, the creative process will take on a life of its own in the purest and most positive sense of the word. It will lead to outstanding results if management doesn't try to impose too many rigid structures on it.

Just as a musician tunes into the central meaning of the song and improvises around that, any great manager or CEO or project leader tunes into the essence of her business or project and lets the rest take care of itself.

She improvises around the chords with feeling and passion. She flows like water and knows that she will achieve outstanding results, even though she may not always know where this process will lead.

You cannot control the process.

The Invisible Hands

This is what I call the "invisible hands." Why? At some point when I'm sitting at the piano and composing, my hands move by themselves. They literally take on a life of their own. I'm sitting there, focusing on bringing an inner vision to life. You cannot control the hands. Surrender to them.

It always takes a bit of courage, but I know I have to trust the process and let the energy flow.

It will take me there, but I have to step back and let the wisdom that simply knows more than I do take over.

The same is true for any business or project, idea or innovative process, in your personal life or in business, whatever your profession may be and whatever area or industry you are in. The basics are always the same, the process is always the same, and the results will always be outstanding if you observe these simple rules.

EXERCISE: Let the Invisible Hands Take Over!
Time needed: 15 minutes

Take any project, idea, service, product, or business that you're working on or planning to start. Size doesn't matter. It is also irrelevant what organization you're in or whether you are your own boss.

Then think of the previous examples and take 15 minutes to try to define the minimum structure that is needed to pull off your project successfully.

Let yourself be guided by this question: "What is *just enough* structure to enable the creative process to happen, but *not too much* structure, in order not to stifle the creative process and suck the life and soul out of it?"

If you have no idea what you need, take your best educated guess. This will get the ball rolling.

Then define where you want to go—your desired outcome.

Focus on this outcome, give yourself up to the creative process, step back, and let the magic happen.

You may have to experiment a little with the structure and adjust it. That's normal. We all do. And you will have to do this again over time as the project develops and unfolds.

Just as a writer has a framework and a routine, and a band needs a studio, people change routines, change studios, and try out different settings and approaches.

Just beware that the number one mistake most people make when they are afraid of the creative process is too much structure. It can be intimidating and exhilarating at the same time to have ideas come out of nowhere, so we all fall prey to "too much structure" at some point.

Remind yourself that you have to let the process flow, and trust in it. This applies equally whether you're a CEO or writing your doctoral dissertation. Remember, the book is the boss. Every project has its own energy. Go with the flow of that energy and trust that it will work out great—and it will!

Step back and let the invisible hands take over. They will take care of the rest. Set the stage, focus on your vision of the ideal outcome, step back, and watch the creative process unfold.

Enjoy the show!

What I love about the creative process, and this may sound naive,
but it is this idea that one day there is no idea, and no solution,
but the next day there is an idea. I find that incredibly exciting.
—Sir Jonathan Ive, designer at Apple Inc.

Points to Remember

Any project, idea, product, service, or business has a life of its own. You have to trust the creative process and let the energy flow. The magic happens when you step back and let the wisdom that simply knows more than you do take over. Set the stage, focus on your vision of the ideal outcome, step back, and watch the creative process unfold.

Trust that the invisible hands, the forces behind any creation or innovation, will take you there. And they will.

The Invisible Radio—Where the World's Greatest Artists (and You!) Get the Best Ideas

Just don't give up trying to do what you really want to do.
Where there is love and inspiration, I don't think you can go wrong.
—Ella Fitzgerald

Eureka! I have found it!
—Archimedes

I was leaving my music studio to go into the kitchen when it hit me. I felt a strong current of energy pulling me back to the piano. Suddenly my hands began to move almost by themselves. A tune formed in my head, and I feverishly started to scribble down lyrics and chords.

The pace was so fast, I could barely keep up with it. After 15 minutes, the song was done.

I gasped. I had tuned in to the "invisible radio," the inner channel that songwriters tune in to to download their songs.

Imagine it as being like a giant inner World Wide Web or your own personal iTunes—the invisible radio with countless unwritten songs. You cannot predict when inspiration will hit you, but if you tune in to that channel, you can be sure it will come. The songs will find you.

This is one of the most fascinating experiences, and it has astounded artists from all over the word for centuries. Nobody knows exactly how it works, but we can surely hear the music.

Any Information Is Available

With the creation of the World Wide Web, we are now living in a world in which there is global connectivity, and information travels instantly. However, we are all connected to an invisible inner web that unites all creation and every single bit of information in the world.

The World Wide Web is an outside replica of this inner world where everything is all one, all connected. This is a world where you can draw any information to you that you desire—past, present, or future.

This is the reason why authors can write about things they have never seen, masterpieces are composed in one's sleep, songwriters hear songs that seemingly come out of nowhere, great inventors can tune in to world-shattering inventions that don't exist yet, and revolutionary products or services are born out of thin air.

This is why a writer like Karl May could write one of the greatest series of Westerns while living in Europe, without ever setting foot in the United States—at a time when there was no Internet or even TV!

Nikola Tesla, the famous inventor, created most of his inventions by playing around with them in his mind before he ever constructed them in real life. He would try them out, take them apart, reconstruct them, and put the pieces back together until they were perfect—all in his mind.

Your Desire Draws the Information to You

Singer and songwriter Daniel Powter was asked in an interview how he composed his world hit "Bad Day." "I was the vessel picking up on the radio frequency," he said.

This invisible radio stores not only creative works of art like paintings, poems, books, songs, and inventions, but also breakthrough ideas for your business, career, products, or services. It also has the best creative solutions to your problems and challenges.

Because you're the vessel, as Daniel Powter put it, you determine which radio frequency you tune in to. Your business or profession, plans and goals, likes and dislikes all determine the kinds of information you attract.

One of the all-time favorite questions that creative people, famous or not, are asked is: "Where do you get your ideas and inspiration from?" The answer is, they keep inner channels open. They tune in to the kind of information they want to receive, then take the pressure off.

Inspiration can come in many forms. It can be a word or sentence you hear in your mind, a sudden urge to go and write something down, a current of energy pulling or pushing you in a certain direction, a sudden inner knowing how the pieces of the puzzle come together, or one of those eureka moments of true breakthrough inspiration.

The desire for the information is the magnet that draws the inspiration into people's lives.

How can you use that to dramatically improve your life, career, or business?

Whatever organization or situation you find yourself in, whatever your skills or your background may be, or whatever solution or idea you are looking for, *any* information is available.

Your desire will draw it to you. It is the magic key that opens the doors to any information.

Keep a Beginner's Mind

> If your mind is empty, it is always ready for anything,
> it is open to everything. In the beginner's mind there are
> many possibilities, but in the expert's mind there are few.
> —Shunryu Suzuki

You don't have to be at the top of your field or industry to receive groundbreaking new ideas, the kind of ideas that can make you a star in your profession.

In the same way that you log on to the web with a computer, you can tap into any information you desire in that inner field of connectivity. Imagine it as being like a giant ocean of information stretching out before you, and you choose.

It's *all there*. This is the belief that you have to acquire; if you don't you will sabotage the radio and distort the frequency. You cannot get any information if you believe that it doesn't exist or that you have no access to it.

A lot of world-shattering inventions were made by amateurs. Why? Because they were more open to new ideas than the experts were.

Consequently, they approached a given challenge, need, or problem with the attitude that there was a new solution out there. They were not confined by dogma or what the experts thought possible.

As a result, they tuned in to the right frequency and picked up on the solution. As Shunryu says in the earlier quote, "In the beginner's mind there are many possibilities, but in the expert's mind there are few."

This is the same process that great entrepreneurs or CEOs use to solve their pressing challenges or create new breakthrough products for their businesses.

What does this mean for you? You have to stay open and receptive, and keep a beginner's mind. Try not to have too many preconceived ideas about the answer or solution you are looking for.

It's All There

No energy is ever lost. No information is ever lost. If someone once had a great idea and didn't act on it further, you can be assured that it's still out there, waiting for you to pick up on it. Capture it. Act on it.

The principal underlying belief that unlocks any information is the belief that it's *all there*.

Likewise, you can pick up on a great idea that somebody else just had. This is the reason why inventions are often made by several people in different parts of the world at the same time.

This is true for start-ups as well. One of my high school friends is Marc Samwer, one of the most successful Internet entrepreneurs in Europe. He was behind the European expansion of eBay and many successful start-ups, and he even holds a personal stake in Facebook.

"There are always different people around the world who have the same or very similar ideas at the same time," Marc says. "This is why execution is king."

Trust Yourself Like a Good Friend That the Answer Will Come to You at the Right Time

Many years ago, I was sitting with Allan Wallace, a meditation teacher and author, on the Big Island of Hawaii. "Allan," I said, "there is a question that has been bugging me for quite some time. What can I do to find the answer?"

"It's simple," Allan replied. "Pose the question to yourself before you meditate. Or you can use some other method to put your mind into a free flow. Then you let go and stay open, receptive, and light about it. But most of all, trust yourself like a good friend that you will bring the answer to yourself at the right time."

I looked at him and smiled.

There were two pearls in this:

1. We have the answers to all our questions. All the information that we desire is there and available to us. This belief will open the gates to all information on this planet and in past and future presents.
2. You have to trust yourself like a good friend that you will bring the information to yourself at the right time. Be patient.

The Dragon in the Cave and the Birth of Luke Skywalker

George Lucas, the creator of the Star Wars saga, once explained how he got the idea for the name of the saga's hero. It happened while he was driving through traffic on the Los Angeles freeway. His mind went into a kind of free flow, he was gazing at the sky, and it hit him: "Luke Skywalker."

James Cameron, the award-winning creator and director of films such as *Titanic* and *Avatar*, says he got the idea for his breakthrough movie, *Terminator*, in a dream when he was 30 and broke.

Many artists get their biggest inspirations when they're showering, driving, relaxing, and letting their mind go into a free flow. In other words, when they are *not* working.

They stay open and receptive, but they are not actively looking for the information. They take the pressure off.

This is the state you want to put yourself into. Define what you want to attract and what kind of information you need, then let go and stay light about it. Don't force it.

The pop group ABBA is undoubtedly one of the most influential, successful, and legendary pop groups of all time. But it was just one of the four members of the group who wrote almost all of the group's songs. He had a great way of describing his creative process. Every day he would dedicate the same hours to "sitting in front of the cave, waiting for the dragon to come out." The dragon, of course, was a new hit song.

"Most days," he went on to say, "the dragon would stay in his cave. But then on some days the dragon would come out, and I would be there and ready, waiting for him."

He knew what he was looking for, and he had clearly defined the outcome: "another hit song." But he waited patiently every day for the same set of hours without putting any pressure on it.

And he succeeded.

Try to copy that process. Adapt it to whatever organization, job, or situation you find yourself in and whatever information you need.

Define the Tools of Your Trade in Order to Slay the Dragon!

> No one was ever great without some portion of divine inspiration.
> —Cicero

When inspiration strikes and the dragon comes out of the cave, you want to be ready.

You need to have the right tools to capture your ideas. The simpler the tools and the lower the maintenance, the better.

As a singer, songwriter, musician, author, speaker, and global entrepreneur, I'm a mixture of old school and high tech. I always carry some sort of recording device with me, plus loads of paper and pens. I also carry a register so that I can scribble down ideas for upcoming meetings, notes to members of my team or partners, and ideas for my projects or businesses. This way, I can sort these things alphabetically right on the spot. It may be a bit old-fashioned, but it works for me.

Take a few sheets of paper and a pen or make sure your iPhone, BlackBerry, or smartphone is charged and ready to receive voice memos or text.

Your Best Inspirations Will Hit You when You Least Expect Them

Like George Lucas driving on the Los Angeles freeway, your greatest and most vital inspirations will come to you precisely when you least expect them—when you take your mind off the problem at hand.

This is why you have to make sure you have your capturing tools ready at all times.

Andrew Lloyd Webber is undoubtedly one of the greatest musical composers of all time. He knows that inspiration can strike at any time. This is why he always carries empty music sheets and a pen with him wherever he goes. This way he can quickly scribble down notes and melodies whenever they come to him.

Against popular belief, the idea that "great inspirations will come back again" is bogus. Andrew still thinks it's necessary to always carry the tools of his trade with him. This is true even after 13 musicals to his credit and countless awards, including seven Tony Awards, three Grammy Awards, and a Golden Globe. You should be wise enough to do the same.

Richard Branson, founder of the Virgin Group, uses a large black notepad that he always carries with him. Many great business ideas have been lost because people have thought, "There's no need for me to capture it now; it'll come back later!"

Some of the greatest inspirations of your life can come and go if you don't have the tools to capture them. If inspiration calls you at 2 a.m., you'd better be ready!

EXERCISE: Define the Tools of Your Trade and Get Ready to Receive

Time needed: 5 minutes

Let's get down to business.

Define the area in which you want to receive your ideas, inspirations, and creative solutions.

This could be in your life, your career, or your business. But I want you to be as precise as possible. Take a sheet of paper and define the question you want answered or the solution you are looking for very clearly. This could also be a new product or service that you want to create.

Then define the tools of your trade. What do you need to have if you are to capture your best ideas when inspiration strikes? Again, the simpler the tools and the lower the maintenance, the better. If a self-made billionaire entrepreneur like Branson uses an old-fashioned notepad and a world-famous composer like Webber uses pen and paper, there's no reason for you to get fancy!

Make a list of your tools now, then make sure you actually get your ducks lined up in a row and carry them with you wherever you go.

Remember, inspiration might call you at 2 a.m., so you'd better get your act together!

As a final step, repeat: "I trust myself like a good friend that this information will come to me in its due time."

We will see you at the cave.

You never have to change anything you got up
in the middle of the night to write.
—Saul Bellow

Points to Remember

The World Wide Web is an outside replica of an inner world where everything is all one, all connected. You can draw any information that you desire to you from that inner field of connectivity—past, present, or future.

Your desire draws the information to you.

You have to stay open and receptive, and keep a beginner's mind. Try not to have too many preconceived ideas about the answer or solution you are looking for.

No energy is ever lost. No information is ever lost. We have the answers to all our questions. All the information we desire is there and available to us. This is the belief that opens the gates to all the information on this planet and in past and future presents.

Define what you want to attract and what kind of information you need, then let go and take the pressure off. You have to trust yourself like a good friend that you will bring the information to yourself at the right time. Be patient.

As a final step, you have to have the right tools to capture your ideas. The simpler the tools and the lower the maintenance, the better.

Step 5

Embrace Change

First the Decision, Then the Prize— How to Create the Ideal Circumstances

Whatever you do, or dream you can, begin it.
Boldness has genius, power and magic in it.
—Goethe

Believe that life is worth living and your belief will create the fact.
—William James

I just got off the phone with one of my best friends, a German DJ and a music producer with a lot of successes under his belt. Whenever we talk, he goes on raving about his dream of relocating to Los Angeles. This has been going on for years now. But, like most other Germans I know, he's waiting for the ideal circumstances to show up before he finally makes a decision and makes the first move. And, of course, those circumstances never come.

Tess Gerritsen, the bestselling novelist, once wrote to me: "You just have to sit down and write. You simply can't wait for the muse."

It's the same with life. You have to make the decision first, and the rest will come.

The 1,000 Helping Hands

I call this phenomenon the 1,000 helping hands.

Think of a rock star giving a concert. He's staring at the glittering lights that are beaming down on him. Suddenly he runs toward the edge of the stage and takes a deep dive into the void—with full faith that he will be saved by the crowd and carried by 1,000 helping hands.

Life *will* carry you. A thousand helping hands *will* show up. But you have to take the dive, that leap of faith; *you* have to decide. *First* you have to make the decision, *then* comes the prize.

It's your decision that sets everything in motion, including life's magical processes and the 1,000 helping hands that will take you toward your goal.

You don't need to have it all figured out. You don't even need to know what the next step will be. Making the decision will be enough, and life will support you with 1,000 helping hands along the way.

Inspiration in Music, Innovation, and the Start of Any New Project or Great Idea

When a musician has an inspiration for a song, he sits down at the piano. The first notes come into his head, an idea. His hands move magically over the keys, music begins to form, and words start to form on paper.

Any creative act takes a leap of faith. The same applies to life in general, to any project or initiative you want to undertake.

Just as lyrics and music seem to come out of nowhere, you have to make a decision and then follow the flow of your impulses, feel your way through it, and trust the process.

The same applies to business and life. Opportunities will arise; the ideal circumstances will come. Life will take you to the fulfillment of your goal. It's the power of your intention and your decision that sets it all into motion. We are taught to wait for the right circumstances before we act. That's an illusion. Reread Goethe's quote at the opening of this chapter, and begin it!

EXERCISE: Do It!

Time needed: 30 seconds

Think back to my German friend. Ask yourself: "What similar decision or big project have I been putting off because I have been waiting for the ideal circumstances to present themselves before I make a decision?"

Stop! Tell yourself: "I am making a decision now. I am acting on my desire and my impulses. I am going for my goals, because I know that when I take a leap of faith and go for what I want, the ideal circumstances will show up in my life, and 1,000 helping hands will be there to support me."

Any good music must be an innovation.
—Les Baxter

I think frugality drives innovation, just like other constraints do.
One of the only ways to get out of a tight box is to invent your way out.
—Jeff Bezos

Points to Remember

Don't wait for the ideal circumstances to take a decision and act. You create the ideal circumstances by making the decision first, then being open to the opportunities that life will present you with.

The ideal circumstances for reaching your goal will come only after you have made your decision, not before.

Life *will* carry you. But you have to take that dive, that leap of faith, and decide. *First* you have to make the decision, *then* comes the prize.

You don't need to have it all figured out. You don't even need to know what the next step will be. It's your decision that sets it all into motion. Life will kick in with its magical processes, and 1,000 helping hands will show up to take you toward your goal and create the ideal circumstances in your life.

The Power of Doing Nothing

Relaxation is an important part of the creative process.
Left alone, you do the right thing.
—Jane Roberts

Sleep is the best meditation.
—The Dalai Lama

I grew up in a culture that's built on BMW efficiency, the principles of German engineering, and doing things according to the book. Most of all, it's a society in which anything that is remotely lazy or that even vaguely resembles "doing nothing" is frowned upon. So it comes as no surprise that "doing nothing" has been challenging for me.

However, we are most creative precisely at those moments when we are not aware of it—the moments when we let our mind go into a kind of free drive.

Our Western societies are saturated with an overflow of information, mental debris, and clutter. We have to consciously weed out the clutter and debris on a continuous basis. This will allow us to feel our impulses more clearly and act on them. And it puts us in touch with the creative genius that we all possess.

Anything Can Be a Meditation

We were sitting together in a half circle at Google headquarters in Silicon Valley, California. I was with my very good friend Meng from Google and U.S. Congressman Tim Ryan. Tim was describing the inexplicable magic that happens when we meditate. We tap into the inner source of our being, and somehow something happens that we cannot quite explain.

Over time, periods of frequent meditation change our internal and external perception and thus our behavior.

We feel a deeper connection with our being and with everything that surrounds us. We feel more embedded in society and in the world at large. We feel more of a connection with our place in the universe, and we have a better understanding of the unique contribution we can make to society.

Meditation is a powerful practice because it lets us tune into our own inner being. Ease and effortlessness are key elements of the practice of meditation.

Contrary to what is commonly thought, anything can be a meditation. We just have to make sure we let our mind go into a kind of free drive at those times. Those periods of free-flowing energy and free-flowing thoughts are essential to reaching our peak potential.

From Surfing to Airplanes

I was with Victor Chan, the founder of the Vancouver Peace Summit, who is also a passionate surfer. We were sitting in a quiet boutique hotel on Manhattan's Lower East Side. Victor explained that, even though he is a devout Buddhist and very adept at traditional meditation, surfing is still his most effective way to meditate: "I really don't meditate that much in the traditional sense of the word, but whenever I get out on the water and windsurf, this is my meditation."

"Doing nothing" can mean many different things to different people. There is no "one size fits all." It could be relaxing in a hammock, looking at the sky, taking a bike ride, lying in the sun—anything that gets you into that kind of mental free flow or drive. For the actor Harrison Ford, flying small airplanes is his unique form of meditation. The singer and songwriter Sting says: "The only meditation I would have done before [yoga] would be in the writing of songs." For the author Stephen King, it's his daily walks on the beach. For the singer Celine Dion—and for a lot of CEOs—it's golf.

There may be things that are considered silly, but that give you true pleasure and satisfaction. Use those activities as a trigger to get into these states of free flow, and engage in them as much as you want.

You Are Most Creative when You Are Not Aware of It—The Invisible Dwarfs

In those periods when you just let go and do "nothing," you open an inner channel that lets your intuitions and impulses come to the fore. This is precisely when the magic happens and you get your best ideas.

Imagine that every time you actually go into a kind of free drive and do nothing, there are a thousand little dwarfs working away who get most active when you're not. This can help you to get out of the traditional mindset and the belief shared by our Western societies that to do more is more.

When we relax, the creativity inside of us is cooking. It is trying to solve our biggest challenges and problems, to produce our biggest and most creative breakthroughs, and to provide insights into the answers we need most.

Capture the Shooting Stars

Alan Wallace is a former professor of religious studies in California and author of more books in English on the benefits of meditation for Western society than any other author. He once told me that he was teaching double the course load of anyone else at Santa Barbara University by incorporating frequent 20-minute periods of meditations into his day. He carried a yoga mat with him all the time so that he could quickly "close the gates" and meditate wherever he was.

Alan also told me that he always has a pen and paper ready during his periods of meditation because some of his greatest ideas come to him during that time.

This is why great composers like Andrew Lloyd Webber always carry a notepad with them to jot down musical ideas that come to their mind during these periods.

You will be likely to produce some of your best ideas during those periods or shortly thereafter. The creativity that will be at work to solve your problems and challenges, both the minor and the major ones, can serve you well only if you actually trust the impulses, intuitions, and ideas that will shoot forth.

Take whatever tools you need to capture them and think of them as being like stars shooting through the night, waiting for you to make the best use of their power and energy.

EXERCISE: Get to Work—Do Nothing!

Time needed: 2 minutes

Make a list of five activities that produce the state of mental free flow or drive that we discussed earlier. Don't wrack your brains over this. These should be activities that come to you with ease, so it shouldn't take more than 30 seconds or a maximum of two minutes to write them down.

It's totally fine to list meditation as one of these activities. But I want you to take a larger look at your life and put down four other activities besides meditation that could serve the same purpose. Of course, we're only looking for activities that have no direct connection to your current job or occupation.

The point of this exercise is to allow you to break free from the traditional concepts of what you think meditation should be like, to get away from a rigid, textbook-style approach to a more personal, individualized one.

This will allow you to be more in touch with your energy and thereby provide the best answers while you go with your own being and experience. Schedule one of these activities now as a private appointment with yourself. Then, over the next weeks, try out all five to see which ones produce the best results.

There's a way to do it better—find it.
—Thomas Edison

Points to Remember

Contrary to what is commonly thought, anything can be a meditation. We just have to make sure we let our mind go into a kind of free drive at those times. Those periods of free-flowing energy and free-flowing thoughts are essential to reaching our peak potential.

There may be things that are considered silly, but that give you true pleasure and satisfaction. Use those activities as a trigger to get into these states of free flow, and engage in them as much as you want.

When we relax, the creativity inside of us is cooking. It is trying to solve our biggest challenges and problems, to produce our biggest and most creative breakthroughs, and to provide insights into the answers we need most.

Life Is Abundance

Abundance is not something we acquire. It is something
we tune into. Doing what you love is the
cornerstone of having abundance in your life.
—Wayne Dyer

The world is full of abundance and opportunity, but far too
many people come to the fountain of life with a sieve
instead of a tank car . . . a teaspoon instead of a steam shovel.
They expect little and as a result they get little.
—Ben Sweetland

I was surfing the net, and I stumbled upon a very intriguing exercise. It was a money exercise that you were to do before you went to sleep.

The exercise was stunningly simple. Before dozing off, when you are lying in bed and the thoughts and worries of the day have subsided, you imagine that there is a bowl of money over your head, right underneath the ceiling. You then imagine the bowl overflowing with money and turning over, and the banknotes falling down to cover your whole body.

You take enough time to feel the money on your skin and try to engage as many of your senses as possible—especially your preferred one. Try to smell, feel, and touch the dollar bills! Indulge in the abundance of having money all around you. Do this for as long as you like. For me, 30 seconds or a minute felt right when I was imagining the whole room filling up with money!

Almost always, I woke up the next morning with the belief that "life is abundance." I could feel that this belief was somehow ingrained much more deeply than at an intellectual level, pervading every cell of my body. Doing this exercise right before sleep had a powerful effect because I was in two worlds at once. I took the feeling of abundance with me into the dream state. As I point out many times throughout this book, the dream state is one of the most powerful tools available to us to create what we want.

I continued to do this every night, and the results were amazing, and not only in my personal finances. I could sense this feeling of abundance working in every area of my life, every single business transaction, and every move I was making, and in a short period of time, my bank account tripled. Opportunities abounded in all areas. I told some of my friends about it, and they applied the exercise with similar results.

An Ocean of Songs, Poems, Paintings, and Business Ideas

Not only did my personal wealth increase, but I also felt my creativity soar.

To put myself into a state where I was at my creative best in music, I gave myself the suggestion that there was an abundance of songs I could tune in to. I literally imagined an ocean of songs out there, waiting to come to life.

This opened up an inner channel. I became extremely receptive to what I call the "invisible radio," the place where not only creative artists but each and every one of us can get their best ideas.

Notes formed magically on paper, my hands moved over the piano, tunes came alive on my lips, lyrics poured out, and I created songs with ease.

I gave myself the same suggestion with poetry, and I could suddenly write a poem a day or even more. I could sense a strong inner connection with a world of creative abundance.

My new belief in abundance was the magic key that opened all doors. I tuned in to that abundance and felt unlimited works of art inside of me longing to come to life.

I then turned to other areas as well, painting being one of them. Before long, I was featured in a book and exhibitions, and 70,000 people saw my paintings.

I discovered that I had always used that belief in abundance to create major breakthroughs in my life in many different areas, not just creativity. But I had not done it consciously, and afterward I had fallen back into society's belief in limitation and lack.

I saw that my new belief in abundance worked for anything, from business ideas to creative solutions to problems or challenges.

The Beginner's Mind in Art, Business, and Life

It dawned on me that this was also the reason why some of humanity's greatest inventions have been made by amateurs. Amateurs approach a problem or need with the mindset that there is an abundance of possible solutions. In the words of Shunryu Suzuki, "In the beginner's mind there are many possibilities, but in the expert's mind there are few."

Experts are so loaded with knowledge in their area that by nature their vision is fenced in—thus, no major breakthroughs are possible.

A beginner's mind approaches a problem, need, or challenge with an unlimited vision—there is literally an abundance of possible solutions. "The amateurs don't know any better!" the experts say.

But a mind that believes in abundance connects you with an ocean of possibilities.

Abundance Is Our Natural State

> If your mind is empty, it is always ready for
> anything, it is open to everything.
> —Shunryu Suzuki

> I keep the telephone of my mind open to . . . abundance.
> Then whenever doubt, anxiety, or fear try to call me,
> they keep getting a busy signal—and soon they'll forget my number.
> —Edith Armstrong

Abundance is our default state of being, our natural state. That means that our being always wants to return to that state.

Our natural impulses and intuitions will lead us to abundance—if we let them. But we have to believe in abundance; if we do not, we will not trust and follow the impulses and natural inclinations that are leading us to it. We have to trust ourselves and our energy.

If you approach anything with a sense of limitation, that's what you will get.

Limiting beliefs are like bars in a prison cell, with the only exception being that they are invisible, so you don't know that you are actually trapped. However, they are there and they are very real when you look for them because their results will show up in your life as a lack of abundance.

Abundance Comes in Many Forms

The state, belief, and mindset of abundance can be applied to any area of your life, of course, not just your personal finances. Abundance comes in many forms. You can have an abundance of health, time, creativity, ideas, solutions, love, and happy relationships—anything that gives you a sense of fulfillment.

Once you adopt the belief that abundance is your natural state, you will magically unlock all doors and opportunities.

The universe is abundance. Any time you are fully immersed in nature and you feel "all one" with the life surrounding you, with shivers running up and down your spine, you can feel and know on a deeper level that the whole universe is abundance and that the only limitations you will find in any area are the ones you create yourself.

Any limitation is based on the underlying belief that there is not enough.

Demand and Supply and Our Biggest Fallacy

Unfortunately, most business schools and universities instill beliefs in their students that are based on limitation. This is constantly reinforced. One of economics' favorite paradigms, the one of supply and demand, is by nature based on a belief in limitation. It promotes a notion of scarcity that pervades modern economics and influences the decisions of policy makers, leading to exactly the kind of scarcity that they ideally want to avoid.

As with everything in life, it's a self-fulfilling prophecy.

No wonder fear abounds in most business schools. Any good student of economics, including myself at the time, would be a fool to renounce the principle of supply and demand and the underlying "truth" of lack and scarcity.

Again, if you look at the full part of the glass, it will change your viewpoint and connect you with a world that is filled with opportunities. They will pop out of nowhere, like mushrooms in an open field of grass after a warm summer rain.

The more you adopt this belief in abundance, the more you will see it manifested in your life and the more you will be able to help others manifest it as well.

EXERCISE: Removing the Invisible Bars of Your Prison Cell

Time needed: 5 minutes

Make two lists.

The first list is a list of limitations. Yes, you heard correctly. I want you to make a list of every single limitation that bugs you in your life.

Then make a second list in which each sentence reads, "There is not enough . . . (money, health, job opportunities, love, business deals, ways to fulfill myself, ways to express myself creatively, ways to start my own business, and so on) in my life."

Now look at both of your lists. Feels pretty miserable, right?

Correct. Now burn the first list (the one with your limitations on it) and repeat, "Life is abundance" and "Abundance is my natural state" while you're looking at the fire. (Be sure to use the kitchen sink, not your living room!)

Turn to your second list. Rewrite each sentence as "There is an abundance of . . . in my life."

Even if you don't believe this at first, do it. (Of course you don't believe it—if you did, it wouldn't be on the list!)

Now reread this new list once a day. Keep doing this even if it gives you an awkward feeling because it goes against what you believe is true. That's the point! We are actively removing the prison bars so that you can step out of your cell of limitation and embrace a world of abundance. It has been right there waiting for you!

Over time, you will see how this new belief and feeling of abundance will expand to touch every area of your life. Prepare yourself to embrace a world filled with opportunities!

EXERCISE: The Money Exercise

Time needed: 30 seconds, right before sleep

This is explained in detail at the beginning of this chapter. Indulge, enjoy, and have fun! This is supposed to be playful.

EXERCISE: The Money Exercise Turbocharged

Time needed: indefinite

To make the money exercise have even more impact, you can bombard your subconscious with images of abundance and wealth throughout the day.

Have someone create mock-up images of abundance in which you paint yourself into the picture. Create fake images that show you in a state of abundance that feels exciting to you and that corresponds to your major goals.

For personal finances, that could be your desk with a pile of cash on top. For creativity, it could show you in a situation where you are performing on a major stage. You might put a painting of yours in a museum with you standing next to it.

Want to start your own business? Why not create an image with the name of your business on top of a big skyscraper or a huge office building?

You are an athlete, and you want to come in first in the next competition? That's easy: put yourself on the top of the pedestal with the trophy in your hand.

You are a CEO and you want to put your company into a market leader position? Have someone Photoshop the logo of your company in the list of the "Best 100 Global Brands" as published by Interbrand and *Bloomberg Businessweek* every year.

Then plaster your home or office with those images.

My wife and I sometimes cover the whole house with images of what abundance means to us to constantly reinforce that belief.

In any case, have fun with it and play with different versions until you find the ones that just "click," the ones that excite you most and send shivers up and down your spine. These are the ones to go with.

Prepare yourself for abundance and keep your arms—and your expectations—wide open!

People with a scarcity mentality tend to see everything in
terms of win-lose. There is only so much; and if someone else has it,
that means there will be less for me. The more we develop
an abundance mentality, the more we believe their success
adds to . . . rather than detracts from . . . our lives.
—Stephen R. Covey

Wherever you are, you are one with the clouds and one with
the sun and the stars you see. You are one with everything.
That is more true than I can say, and more true than you can hear.
—Shunryu Suzuki

Points to Remember

Abundance is our natural state.

If you approach anything with a sense of limitation, that's what you will get.

It's all in the mind: If you adopt a belief in abundance, it will change all areas of your life, not just your personal finances. It will connect you with a world that is filled with opportunities. They will pop out of nowhere, like mushrooms in an open field of grass after a warm summer rain.

A mind that believes in abundance will unlock an ocean of possibilities, and a million doors will open that you did not even know existed. The more you adopt this belief in abundance, the more you will see it manifested in your life and the more you will be able to help others manifest it as well.

Sharon Stone and Kung Fu Balance

Imagine life as a game in which you are juggling some balls
in the air. You name them—Work, Family, Health, Friends and Spirit—
and you're keeping all of these in the air. You will soon understand
that work is a rubber ball. If you drop it, it will bounce back. But the
other four balls are made of glass. If you drop one of these,
they will be irrevocably scuffed, marked, nicked, damaged
or even shattered. They will never be the same.
—Brian Dyson, former CEO of Coca-Cola Enterprises

Wishes are served on a silver plate,
dare to dream,
get carried away by the sound of your own inner magic.
We will be there, the gods of your presence,
when you feel what you love
and love what you do,
for life is made for you to mold it,
and love is life to be lived.
—Lyrics of my song "Free Your Mind" from the
Café del Mar 25th Anniversary album

I was in Venice Beach, California. When I woke up, the surfers were already in full play. That afternoon, I was to have my first meeting with Sharon, who wanted to get involved in my World Peace Foundation.

I told my PA not to schedule any other meetings for that day and did what I love: I rented a surfboard and hit the water.

When Sharon walked into the restaurant of the Beverly Hills Hotel later that day, dazzling and glamorous, it didn't feel like work at all. In fact, none of the next few days did. I kept my perfect balance, hit the waves, jogged on the beach, attended cool arts exhibitions and gallery openings, and met friends for dinner.

In hindsight, this was the wisest thing I could have done. It put me in a frame of mind that was constructive, relaxed, and utterly in balance.

During the next couple of days, my wishes were served on a silver platter. Sharon and I totally hit it off. We brainstormed about all the different ways in which she could support my foundation, from organizing fundraisers to getting Hollywood actors and world-famous artists on board. She was the real deal.

After a relaxed afternoon at her house and a dinner with some of her best friends, we hugged and looked forward to doing great things together.

"And we will," she said, with a smile, before we waved goodbye.

When Work Doesn't Feel Like Work, You're on the Right Track

No wonder I got the best results. There's a certain magic that happens when you respect your balance 100 percent. Life produces the best outcomes and wildly surpasses your expectations with ease.

I've since learned that when work doesn't feel like work, you'd better keep doing what you're doing. That's when you produce your best results. When you are in balance, life serves you your wishes on a silver platter. It's effortless.

After those days in California, I took an early red-eye flight to New York City. My first meeting started at 6:30 a.m., after just two hours of sleep.

This set the pace for the whole week. Insanity ruled. Balance always has to be your number one priority, but in this situation, I made all the wrong moves. I didn't listen to my intuition, overscheduled my days, and quickly got out of balance.

Meeting after meeting with no downtime put me in a state of mind where I was not able to hear, focus on, or follow my intuitions and impulses. When my inner voice shouted: "After New York City, take the next flight back to Los Angeles and tie the knot on everything you planned with Sharon!," I didn't listen. Even when I heard that inner voice again and again, I still didn't listen. My impulses were as straightforward as if Arnold Schwarzenegger were hitting me over the head with a sledgehammer.

How It All Went to Hell—and What You Can Learn from It

I missed out on a major opportunity when I didn't take up Sharon's suggestion that I go back to California and sit down with her to tie the knot on everything we had planned. Instead, I listened to members of my team, who told me that I should fly back to Europe and that I could follow up on everything that Sharon and I had discussed via phone or e-mail.

As it turned out, Sharon and I clicked best when we actually sat down together in person—as is the case with so many people. Being overworked and totally out of balance, I didn't manage to pull off the next steps that were needed to complete the right follow-up.

The old excuse "I will save time and money" made me lose one of the most important opportunities for my foundation at that time. In hindsight, this single move could have saved me two years of work on that project.

Never underestimate the importance of balance for producing your best results with ease.

Life usually presents you with the best and most direct way to reach your goals. Then it is up to you to take the initiative, act on your impulses, and seize those opportunities.

Kung Fu Balance: The Horse Stance

> Don't think. Feel! It's like a finger pointing to
> the moon. Don't concentrate on the finger
> or you'll miss all that heavenly glory.
> —Bruce Lee

> In all my years of counseling those near death, I've yet to hear
> anyone say they wish they had spent more time at the office.
> —Rabbi Harold Kushner

Kung fu teaches you what it takes to be in balance. If you are not firmly grounded, your opponent will strike you down with a single punch.

The stance of your legs and the positioning of your lower body are key. This is what we call the "horse stance."

It takes its name from the position assumed when riding a horse: you gently lower your body's center of gravity by bending your knees while keeping your back straight.

For my black belt in Korean kung fu, I had to learn this the hard way. After endless blows and dislocated shoulders and feet, I finally got it. The major advantage of this position is that your opponent cannot easily get you off balance. Masters at this art are so firmly grounded with their legs and feet that it is hard for even three opponents to change their position. There are demonstrations in Asia where kung fu masters are attacked by as many as ten different opponents at the same time and still do not give way an inch.

In martial arts, you have to be firmly grounded in order to have the full strength of your body available. In the same way, in business and in life, balance will put you in a position where you have the full force of your skills, talents, and intuitions available. This way you can react swiftly, with ease and high concentration, to any challenges or opportunities that come up.

The biggies, the opportunities that take you toward your goals in major quantum leaps, may come to you with ease, but it takes a truly balanced mind to recognize them and bring them home.

Take Away the Noise

I could have called this section "Overworking, Balance, and Intuition." If you're overworked and out of balance, you won't have access to your intuition and your own inner guidance system.

When you are out of balance, you get into a situation in which there is too much noise. Compare this to a radio that's tuned to the wrong frequency. You get a lot of clutter and static along with the main program. If you're overworked and out of balance, you will not be able to hear your own intuition correctly, as if you were trying to listen to a wise man sitting next to you who was whispering in your ear while you were in heavy traffic. It's the worst thing you can do to block your success. The faster you can get out of that state, the better. This will put you into a position where you will work smart, not hard.

Obama on Balance

Let the president have the final word. Here's what Barack Obama said in a Q&A on Reddit in August 2012 as a response to the question: "How do you balance family life and hobbies with being the POTUS?"

> It's hard—truthfully the main thing other than work is just making sure that I'm spending enough time with Michelle and the girls. The big advantage I have is that I live above the store—so I have no commute! So we make sure that when I'm in DC I never miss dinner with them at 6:30 p.m.—even if I have to go back down to the Oval for work later in the evening. I do work out every morning as well, and try to get a basketball or golf game in on the weekends just to get out of the bubble. Speaking of balance, though, I need to get going so I'm back in DC in time for dinner.

If the president can do it, with the insanely busy schedule he has and the million demands on his time, so can you. No more excuses!

EXERCISE: Your Horse Stance for Maximum Results

Time needed: 3 minutes

Balance means that you are firmly grounded so that anything that comes your way and anything that is unforeseen, whether it's a fantastic new opportunity, a small blip, or a catastrophe, will not catch you off guard. It will never upset your balance. You will have a "mind like water" and a horse stance like a true kung fu master. If this sounds unreal or too difficult to attain, it isn't, because we all have an inner compass that leads us back to our balance naturally once we listen to it and give it room.

Balance is defined in its own unique way for each and every one of us. Sit down and make a list of what balance means to you.

Make a list of the things that are absolutely crucial for keeping your balance. This is your baseline. I know some very successful entrepreneurs who need half an hour each day at the keyboard or piano to be fully balanced, to be able to tune in to their intuitions correctly, even though they are not professional musicians. Balance is a unique mix. For me, it's getting my naps in every day, meditating, expressing my creativity for a certain number of hours, going to bed no later than 10:30 or 11 at night, and getting in an hour and a half of sports every day. If I guard this balance religiously, then I can create great results with ease. At the same time, this balance ensures that I have enough high-quality time with myself, my friends, and my family, and that my overall social life is fulfilled.

What If You Don't Know What Balance Means to You?

It may take you some time to find out what truly matters in creating an ideal balance in your life. Try to imagine that you are a kung fu fighter, legs and feet firmly rooted to the ground, relaxed, eyes slightly closed, ready to face your opponent at any moment.

This exercise will serve as a kick-start to get you away from the totally overworked and unproductive lifestyle that most people in our modern civilized world lead. Just brainstorm away and keep adding to your list until it feels right. Then put it to the test and adjust it.

Your list of the basic elements of your balance should be the cornerstone of your daily diary and agenda planning. I've set myself up in such a way that my assistant has the list ready and knows my routine by heart. She plans every day accordingly. For example, no calls are ever scheduled in the morning because that's my time for meditation, creativity, and sports. We deviate from this schedule only in times of absolute emergency, if I have to give a keynote speech at noon or hop on a plane in the morning, for example.

Work from the inside out and define what it means for you to be in balance and thereby produce outstanding and phenomenal results, the kind of results that will help you reach your full potential and will set you apart from others in your own unique way. Then bring in anything else that's important and that imposes limitations on your schedule from the outside. In the end, it will be a mix of the two.

What happens with most people is that they cater exclusively to the demands of their working environments, adjusting their schedules accordingly but failing to integrate the needs of their own individual balance. Consequently, they are overworked, produce mediocre results, are very unhappy, and never come even close to realizing their true potential. What remains is an underlying sense of incompletion and an inner vacuum that they try to fill by working even more, which obviously makes things worse. Quit the hamster wheel and get into your kung fu stance!

> I could dramatically improve your financial success
> by giving you a card with 20 holes in it, representing the
> total of all financial investments you could make over your lifetime.
> —Warren Buffett

Points to Remember

There's a certain magic that happens when you respect your balance 100 percent. When work doesn't feel like work, you produce your best results. When you are in balance, life serves you your wishes on a silver platter and wildly surpasses your expectations with ease.

Never underestimate the importance of balance for producing your best results with ease.

Life usually presents you with the best and most direct way to reach your goals. Then it is up to you to take the initiative, act on your impulses, and seize those opportunities. In business and in life, balance will put you in a position where you have the full force of your skills, talents, and intuitions available.

With a balanced mind, you will be in a position to recognize the big opportunities that will take you toward your goals in major quantum leaps *and* to bring them home.

Your Hour of Power

> I don't have delusions of grandeur,
> I have an actual recipe for grandeur.
> —Eddie Morra in *Limitless*

There exist limitless opportunities in every industry.
Where there is an open mind, there will always be a frontier.
—Charles F. Kettering

The MBA program director came to me after one of my lectures. "You know the Hour of Power you talked about? I did it, and it works! It gets me out of the hecticness of the day. It gets me back to where I want to go. I focus on what I want, set my course, and recharge my energy. It's amazing how one hour a day can have such a powerful effect and radically change your life!"

The Hour of Power is one of the all-time favorite exercises among my global MBA students.

It's an hour you take for yourself each day, ideally in the morning before your day begins.

Use it to:

- Remind yourself of your greatest successes
- Review the praise you have received from others
- Look at positive, constructive, and uplifting beliefs you have collected
- Look at your vision board that depicts the scene of your ideal future
- Fall in love with mock-up images of yourself being, doing, and having what you want, including inner and outer success and happiness, wealth, goals, and accomplishments

It also includes a time set aside for visualization exercises. Close your eyes, listen to music, and repeat suggestions to yourself so that you can imagine the vision of your ideal future as if it existed already in the here and now.

During this period of time, it is important to remind yourself that you can grow into that future as easily as you grew from the past into the present. We have lost the sense of ease in today's world, so it is important that you reclaim it and remind yourself of the ease and the effortlessness of creating your ideal future again and again.

Become Limitless

I also use this hour to meditate for at least 10 to 15 minutes. It's funny how the concept of the Hour of Power universally applies to everyone. I see people benefiting from it in fantastic ways. Each person uses the hour in his or her own unique way. For an MBA director, it becomes part of her daily walk from home to work. A Middle Eastern student retreats to the mosque to meditate. Others do exactly as I just described: look at their vision board, lie down, close their eyes, and imagine their ideal future.

How you want to play it is up to you. You know by now that I am opposed to a "one-size-fits-all" strategy and game plan. I would much rather offer you a bundle of different possibilities and let you take your pick. You can trust yourself, like a good friend, to find what's right for you.

The basic concept remains: take one hour each day—ideally at the beginning of each day, the earlier the better—to indulge in your own personal *me* time. This is just for you and no one else. Shut out all distractions, close the doors, and say goodbye to your family, friends, or children.

For me, this is sacred time: no e-mail, no phone, no TV, no Internet, no nothing. Just me, myself, and I.

Become Your Own Harry Potter

Our world is magical, and most things are a lot easier than you think because they are about as easy as you make them. This personal Hour of Power will protect you. It will serve as a shield against the negative beliefs in limitation and lack that pervade our society.

This is why I recommend that you include a collection of praise that you have received, large or small, from anybody in your life. Put it all down on a sheet of paper or on your laptop or smartphone, so that you can review it for as long as you want during your Hour of Power.

Just looking at praise, even if it wasn't given to you personally, has an amazing effect. Dan Ariely, who is a professor of behavioral science at Duke University, published a great app that is called "At a boy!" At the touch of a button, it sends you a never-ending stream of praise and uplifting remarks.

This app is great, but it's even better to make a list of personal praise you have actually received because it will resonate with you more, will have more meaning, and therefore will have a bigger impact.

We live in a society and have an educational system that largely focuses on our mistakes, our faults, and our character flaws instead of on our personal assets, skills, talents, strengths, and successes. I want you to rebuild your own self-image from the bottom up. To this end, I want you to look at the half-full part of the glass when it comes to your character, life, talents, and unique strengths and abilities. This is why the collection of praise is so important.

Create Success by Building on Your Past Successes

> We do not need magic to transform our world. We carry
> all of the power we need inside ourselves already.
> —J. K. Rowling

> Wisdom is the accumulation of feelings of success.
> —José Silva

I also want you to pat yourself on the back when it comes to your successes. Here we often fall prey to another bad habit. We think of "successes" in terms of larger-than-life successes—the Big Hairy Audacious Goals, the top 10 of our life, the Everest mountaintops.

It is great to motivate yourself by focusing on your ultimate goals. But when it comes to your successes, pat yourself on the back for every single positive accomplishment, no matter how small. "Did another session at the gym"; pat yourself on the back. "Made that sales call"; pat yourself on the back. "Helped a friend in need"; pat yourself on the back. Everything counts. Put it all down.

List all these things in a table of successes (I put quick notes in my smartphone), and review it regularly during your Hour of Power. You will be amazed at how your self-image changes radically, and with it your life and your success in business. You will reach your personal "Superman" status in no time. The sky's the limit, baby!

Then it won't be long before actual Superman results show up in your life.

I know very talented people who, when they go to bed at night, list their numerous failures and mistakes during the day. This doesn't get you anywhere. You can be the greatest genius of your time, but if you continue to put yourself down like that, you will feel that you are caught in a quicksand of fear and self-destruction.

The only way to transform your self-image, transform your life, and transform your success in business is to bombard yourself with a never-ending stream of positive suggestions, imagery, praise, visions, desires, goals, and successes.

EXERCISE: Getting Your Ducks in a Row
Time needed: 20 minutes

Let's review. You need a vision board that contains images, cutouts from magazines, mock-up images, or photographs of things you want to have, be, or become. This can include the inner world as well as the outer, from happiness and personal fulfillment to cash, a house on the beach, a big fat bank account, and a life where you are surrounded by friends and admirers.

Don't forget areas like your body and personal fitness! In the section in this book called "The Big-Wave Surfer Meets Google—Use All Your Senses and Skyrocket to Success," I talk at length about the benefits of taking good care of your body and listening to it. It is your top decision-making tool to realize your true potential, choose the best opportunities, and become a high achiever in whatever area, industry, or profession you wish.

Add a sheet of paper headed "Successes," another sheet headed "Praise," and another sheet headed "Positive and Constructive Beliefs." On the last one, list any positive statements or uplifting beliefs that you read, hear about, get in contact with, or come up with yourself.

Then add a description of the vision of your ideal future (discussed in the section "The Power of Your Personal Vision").

Put all of this in a folder. Done and dusted!

Your Shopping Mall

I am going to let you in on a little secret. I see the world as a giant shopping mall, a gateway to my ideal future. It's a mall of never-ending future possibilities where I can go and pick whatever I want. In doing that, I collect images of whatever I want to acquire, have, be, or become and put it in my folder. This way, my subconscious mind goes to work on it, and my whole being will conspire with the universe to help me achieve that reality.

It's that simple. Look on the world as a giant supermarket. Take your pick. You can be or become whatever you put your mind to and focus on.

The Internet is the easiest place in the world to shop for images of your ideal future. Your mind and your subconscious are convinced by little things. There's no need to go for perfection. A simple cutout of your head on that gorgeous new body you want is enough, or a cutout of yourself placed in your ideal house, happy family, ideal life, or dream job.

Want to get it perfect? Get someone to Photoshop you into that dream job, new company, or ideal lifestyle.

I couldn't resist Photoshop, and it works great for me. But the most amazing bodily transformation I ever accomplished was done by focusing on a simple cutout of my face on a gorgeous new body that I printed from the web. We're all kids, after all. The simple things that worked back then still do. We just feel so compelled to behave like adults all the time!

Remember, you get what you focus on. Your Hour of Power is the place and time that you need if you are to build an image of yourself in the most fulfilled reality that you can experience. It's the fastest and most direct way for you to manifest that reality.

The Hour of Power is your number one power booster to radically improve your life, your career, or your business.

Points to Remember

The only way to transform your self-image, transform your life, and transform your success in business is to bombard yourself with a never-ending stream of positive suggestions, imagery, praise, visions, desires, goals, and successes.

The Hour of Power is an hour you take for yourself each day, ideally in the morning before your day begins. Use it to visualize your ideal future.

Remind yourself that you can grow into this ideal future as easily as you grew from the past into the present.

Remember, you get what you focus on. Your Hour of Power is the place and time that you need if you are to build an image of yourself in the most fulfilled reality that you can experience. It's the fastest and most direct way for you to manifest that reality.

The Hour of Power is your number one power booster to radically improve your life, your career, or your business.

Step 6

Overcome Your Challenges

Overcome Self-Doubt for Good and Skyrocket to Success

Even though I walk through the valley of the
shadow of doubt, I will fear no evil.
—Paraphrase of Psalm 23:4

There is nothing more dreadful than the habit of doubt.
—The Buddha

The Girl from Afar

Let me take you back many years.

I was sitting on the beach in the South of France on a hot August day, having very human doubts. I was putting the finishing touches on my master's thesis in economics, and I had been admiring this Italian girl from afar for the last three days. It had become unbearable torture. By now, I was idealizing her like a Greek goddess!

I finally mustered the strength to go over and talk to her. In two minutes, the Greek goddess I had been fantasizing about had vanished, and my attraction went to zero.

What I regretted most were the three days I had wasted, caught up in my self-doubts, instead of just acting on my impulses and walking up to her.

We Are Not Born with Self-Doubt

Fast-forward: the Dalai Lama and a group of Tibetans were meeting Western scientists in California. A psychologist raised a question: "Your Holiness, how do you deal with self-doubts?" The Dalai Lama looked puzzled and asked his interpreter for help. The interpreter did his best, but the Dalai Lama still looked surprised, as if he didn't understand the question.

The truth was: he didn't. There is a word for doubt in the Tibetan language, but there's no word for self-doubt. It simply doesn't exist. The Dalai Lama turned to his fellow Tibetans and asked: "Do any of you know what that is, self-doubt? Has any of you had any experience with this?" They shook their heads.

We are not born with self-doubt.

Our Western society, education, and culture teach us to cultivate self-doubt as we are growing up. Self-doubt is simply a culturally acquired habit, nothing more and nothing less. This is good news because it means that we can actually *unlearn* it, just as we can unlearn any other habit.

What really distinguishes people who get things done and realize their dreams from others is that they don't allow their self-doubts to stop them. Or, as Buddha said, they don't cultivate the "habit of doubt."

Self-Doubt and a High IQ

In my work and interaction with countless individuals from all educational, racial, ethnic, and social backgrounds around the globe, I've seen that in most societies, self-doubt is a common cultural phenomenon.

Unfortunately, in those societies, self-doubt is also often a by-product of a superior intellect. If you're more intelligent, it's easier to doubt yourself.

The reason for this is simple: we have been trained to use our intellect to compare ourselves to others and to see where we come up short. Using our intellect in this erroneous way means that we find more of the little and big faults in ourselves, downplay our successes, and emphasize our failures and our lack of accomplishments.

People with less talent or intellect are more courageous when it comes to taking the stage—anywhere, anytime.

Going back to the girl from afar example, most guys certainly have their fair share of stories like that: the guy with no brains walks right up to the girl and starts a conversation because he doesn't doubt himself, while we are still thinking about the perfect pickup line and the right approach.

We admire rock stars who go out on stage because of their boldness, their courage, and their ability to stand up for themselves and live their dreams. We admire them because they are chasing their dreams without letting self-doubt stop them. They act in *spite* of doubt.

I still remember the very first time I saw Madonna perform at the Oscars. Her hands were shaking, but she still went out there and put on a great show.

Use Positive Imagery

What has helped me a lot in dealing with self-doubts and unlearning this dreadful habit is the image of water flowing in a river. The stones in the river are the doubts. Don't try to get rid of them. Flow around them the way the river flows around the stones.

The stones are part of the river, but the river doesn't let them stop the flow of its water. Don't try to pretend that your self-doubts are not there. Instead, simply don't pay any attention to them and follow the natural flow of your energy.

This way, they will have no power over you, and you won't waste your time or energy trying to get rid of them.

Focus on your goals, your ideal scene, your dreams and aspirations. They can be compared to the river's final destination: the ocean.

When you focus on reaching the ocean, your goals and dreams, you let your natural energy flow freely. And then life's natural rhythms will take you there just as surely as the river flows to the ocean. It's that simple.

EXERCISE: Visual Trigger—Free the River

> Can you imagine what I would do if I could do all I can?
> —Sun Tzu

Time needed: 15 seconds

Next time you catch yourself in a situation where you are damming up the river by impeding the flow of your energy, doubting yourself, or second-guessing yourself, make a "swooping" gesture with your hand as if you were wiping your doubts away.

This practice will serve as a physical trigger to take action and not let your doubts stop you. It will remind you to act in *spite* of self-doubts.

Before long, this will become second nature, and you too will take to the stage and live your dreams without stopping yourself.

EXERCISE: Walk Through the Valley of the Shadow of Doubt and Fear No Evil!

Time needed: whatever is necessary to express yourself and get you back into a positive state

What does it mean to "walk through" your doubts?

If you have self-doubts, you can't deny them; that won't work. It will only impede your energy. Instead, objectify them. This will enable you to live *through* the unpleasant feelings without denying them or giving them more room than they deserve. It will channel them into something constructive.

Then you will see that they have no more power over you. On the contrary, this practice will free you up to take constructive action.

Musicians and creative artists know that *any* energy can be converted into something constructive.

The blues is a prime example. Musicians who play the blues use their moods as a rich bed of creativity, a springboard for creating beautiful masterpieces that inspire us all. I'm sure you remember a tune that just about expresses how you are feeling when you are in a lousy mood and caught up in self-doubts. Sing that song. Make up your own. Express yourself! You will automatically feel better.

Writers put their feelings on paper. You can use the same method by just making a journal entry, spilling your guts and telling the blank page how much life sucks right now. Objectify your self-doubts by putting them all on paper.

Painters use dark colors to show themselves and the world how they are feeling. Take a pencil and a sheet of paper and draw that lousy mood, draw those doubts. This is not supposed to be a masterpiece, and you certainly don't have to show it to anyone.

Remind yourself that some of life's greatest breakthroughs happen precisely after the moments of deepest doubt, despair, or depression— you have to walk through the valley of the shadow of doubt to get to the other side.

EXERCISE: Take to the Stage!

Time needed: 2 minutes

Think back to an episode in your personal life when somebody else acted on an impulse you had while you were still busy doubting and second-guessing yourself. (The rival in the attractive girl/boy example is always a good one.)

Alternatively, think of an episode when you lost a valuable opportunity simply because you waited too long before you started to act, caught up in self-doubts and blocking your course of action.

How could boldness have helped you in either of these cases? How could you have reacted differently and produced much better results?

Now close your eyes and try to imagine that different, more ideal outcome of the situation.

You have just taken a powerful step toward taking to the stage, even though your hands may be shaking like Madonna's at the Oscars. You have trained your mind and your subconscious to act boldly on your impulses next time and take action toward your goal!

When you don't know what to do, act as if you do.
—Anthony Robbins

Points to Remember

We are not born with self-doubt. But our society, education, and culture teach us to cultivate self-doubt as a necessary habit. Self-doubt is simply a culturally acquired habit, nothing more and nothing less. This is good news because it means that, as with any other habit, we can *unlearn* it.

What really distinguishes people who get things done and realize their dreams from others is that they don't allow their self-doubts to stop them. They act *in spite* of their doubts.

If you have self-doubts, you can't deny them. This will only impede your energy. Instead, objectify them. This will enable you to live *through* the unpleasant feelings without giving them more room than they deserve. It will channel them into something constructive.

Some of life's greatest breakthroughs happen precisely after the moments of deepest doubts, despair, or depression. You have to walk *through* the valley of the shadow of doubt to get to the other side.

How to Turn Every Failure into Victory

It is impossible to live without failing at something,
unless you live so cautiously that you might as well
not have lived at all—in which case, you fail by default.
—J. K. Rowling

You fail if you don't try. If you try and you fail, yes, you will have a
few articles saying you've failed at something. But if you look at the
history of American entrepreneurs, one thing I do know about them: An awful
lot of them have tried and failed in the past and gone on to great things.
—Richard Branson

I still remember the first time I watched J. K. Rowling's Harvard commencement speech on YouTube. It was titled "The Fringe Benefits of Failure, and the Importance of Imagination."

Never before had I heard anyone talk about failure the way she did:

So I think it fair to say that by any conventional measure, a mere seven years after my graduation day, I had failed on an epic scale. An exceptionally short-lived marriage had imploded, and I was jobless, a lone parent, and as poor as is possible to be in modern Britain, without being homeless. . . . By every usual standard, I was the biggest failure I knew. . . .

So why do I talk about the benefits of failure? Simply because failure meant a stripping away of the inessential. I stopped pretending to myself that I was anything other than what I was, and began to direct all my energy into finishing the only work that mattered to me. Had I really succeeded at anything else, I might never have found the determination to succeed in the one arena I believed I truly belonged. I was set free, because my greatest fear had already been realized.

The rest is history. She created the Harry Potter fantasy series, which has sold more than 400 million copies to become the bestselling book series ever. And on top of it, her books have inspired younger generations and millions of computer game kids to take up reading again—an outstanding accomplishment in its own right.

How My Biggest Failure Led Me Back to What I Loved Most

I was sitting at my desk, sweating. One of my companies was in deep trouble. I had reached what Italians call the giorno buio, the dark day.

Looking back, my failure was inevitable because I had been overworked and out of balance. I hadn't listened to my intuition, and I had put the wrong people in charge. When my inner voice told me to fire them, I still didn't listen. I was grateful to have a helping hand, even if it was the wrong one.

From a larger perspective, this became rock bottom for me. But just as J. K. Rowling describes, it led me back to what I loved. I realized that what I really wanted to do was to spend my time focusing on the things that truly mattered to me, my greatest passions. My role in the company that I had created just wasn't for me. I would have done much better putting someone else in charge; I should have been its visionary, not its CEO.

Almost Every Seeming Tragedy Contains a Gift in Disguise

You have to trust in yourself, and you have to trust in life. As my friend Rick Stack, an entrepreneur and author, likes to say: "Go with the flow and trust that everything will work out great for you, and it will!"

The problem is that a lot of people keep dwelling on misery and tragedies, and so they never get out of the hole. They dig their own mental pit and continue digging. That certainly doesn't work.

Rick told me another great story. He was living in New York City with his wife in a wonderful apartment right next to Central Park. Then the landlord informed him that they had to move out. They were devastated. They didn't really want to live anywhere else, but then again they were expecting a child, so after giving it considerable thought, they finally gave in. In the end, the owner had to buy them out and made them a great offer that reduced their rent for the last 10 to 15 years to virtually zero. At the same time, they moved to a place that was just 15 minutes outside the city, but was a much better environment for their child to grow up in. Looking back, this was the best and the smartest choice. Not only did they save a lot of money, but they ended up being much happier, and they found just the right place for them and for their new family. Again, you can't connect the dots looking forward, but you have to trust that things will work out great for you, and they will.

Failures Set Us Up for Our Biggest Successes

I was sitting at a dinner table in London with a group of fellow members of the Global Philanthropists Circle. Mads Skaer, a Norwegian entrepreneur, said: "Tom, don't you think it's funny how entrepreneurs and business leaders usually don't like to talk about their failures? Yet our failures produce some of our biggest insights and often create even greater opportunities."

Rewind to many years earlier. I had once hit an all-time financial low. On top of that, my car had broken down and I couldn't afford to repair it.

I remembered an exercise that my friend Marc Allen had talked about in his book *The Millionaire Course*. I made a list of 15 things that could come out of this situation that would be beneficial. While I was riding my bike, I could get a great workout on my way to the gym and discover new areas of the city. I could use public transportation and stay at a friend's place in another city if I wanted to go out on the weekend, and this would allow me to spend more time with my friend. I stretched my imagination to come up with a list of every possible positive thing that could come out of this situation and put it on index cards.

I reviewed this list every day until I was less depressed by the situation. As a result, I got myself some breathing time; the situation didn't look so bad after all. When my perspective started to change, it wasn't long before I managed to turn my financial situation around.

I then started to apply this exercise to other areas of my life as well, with amazing results. Our life changes with our viewpoint and the beliefs we focus on. The funny thing is that the opportunities were there all along; we just don't see them unless we change our beliefs and perspective.

This is a mundane example, but it works if you hit a financial low or are even hitting rock bottom and living below the poverty line, as J. K. Rowling was. As Richard Branson says, "If you focus obsessively on opportunities you can turn any seeming failure around."

Embrace Failure and Unwrap the Gifts

In hindsight, most of the seeming tragedies in our lives are really the things that set us up for our biggest successes. It takes courage to remind ourselves of that when we're down and out. But we have to be willing to unwrap the gifts. They are waiting under the Christmas tree, but if we're looking in the wrong direction, we will never see them.

Therefore, when you find yourself in a seeming dilemma or dire situation, ask yourself: "What are the fringe benefits here? What are the opportunities?"

I remember reading a story about a man who died, was reanimated, and came back to life. He described making the transition to the other side as one of the most beautiful experiences he had ever had, and said that he had been welcomed by a group of wise men who shared some of the essential secrets of life with him. When he came back to life and was unable to put this experience into words, he summed it up in one: "Yes!"

Eckhart Tolle, the author of *The Power of Now*, one of the bestselling books of the last decade, says that when he was hitting an all-time low and wanted to kill himself, an inner voice told him to just go with the flow of life and say yes to it.

When problems come up, you still have to say yes to the situation; you have to go with it. Going with it means being one with life's energy in the moment, and being one with your spontaneous being. Trusting your instincts and impulses along with changing your viewpoint will show you the way.

Most of our failures are really blessings in disguise. They are gift packages that we have to unwrap. However, we have to be willing to change our perspective and see them in that light.

Try on the opportunity glasses. Since life is abundance, they will guide you in the right direction. Then the biggest successes are often just right around the corner.

Prepare Yourself for Your Rebound and Your Second Wind

A good friend of mine is a legendary surfer and waterman from Maui who truly turned himself into an icon at the height of his career. He inspired millions of people around the world to pick up a surfboard. However, he wasn't a good businessman. During his career, he was exploited by some of the major surf brands, including the ones that he had helped to make world-famous. However, he was still living comfortably on the earnings from his former career and getting ready to embark on a new adventure and a new business path. Then it happened: he hit another all-time low. Because of a failed marriage, he basically lost everything he had and was left with nothing. He fell into depression for years. I told him again and again to remember that giant within, his own unique energy that had been powerful enough to turn him into a legend in sports. I told him that he could use this massive energy constructively to reach whatever goal he wanted, including getting himself out of this all-time low, desolate financial state, and depression.

One day he sent me a video of a new film he was in. It was a trailer that announced a revolution in surfing and showed him performing some of the craziest moves on a stand-up paddle board the world had ever seen, including the first three-meter aerials.

He recently sent me another picture of him placing second between a 16-year-old and a 23-year-old, both of whom are considered to be among the best surfers in the world. My friend had just turned 50, so you can imagine the smile on his face. When I asked him how he had pulled it off, he said, "You keep telling me it's all in the mind, and that's exactly what I repeated to myself over and over again. Repeating this suggestion over and over again allowed me to reach my all-time high."

Everything and anything can be a blessing in disguise, but we have to be open to it, listen to our own inner guidance system, and trust in life's magical processes.

Billy Joel, the famous American singer and songwriter, wrote his song "Second Wind" to provide encouragement for teenagers in depression. Without further ado, grab Billy's song and listen to it when you find yourself in one of those rough spots.

EXERCISE: Turn Every Failure into Victory

Step 1: The Basics
Time needed: 3 minutes

Take an episode from the past or present that you would describe as a failure, maybe even a tragedy. Then take a sheet of paper or a set of index cards and try to come up with 15 great things that could or could have come out of this seeming tragedy or failure. Brainstorm and stretch your imagination. This exercise alone will make you adopt a different viewpoint that will lead you to discover the blessings, gifts, opportunities, and potential victories in any given situation. Even if the real opportunity is not contained in your list yet, this exercise will set the processes in motion that will bring about a change in your perception and, as a result, your reality.

Step 2: Take It a Step Further: The Persistently Positive Perspective
Time needed: 3 minutes

If you have the time, take another three minutes to take this a step further. Ask yourself: "What if this was the biggest and best opportunity that has ever happened to me? How would I reinterpret the situation? And what would that opportunity be?"

Look at it as if your whole world, yourself included, had conspired to bring about this situation to set you up for your biggest breakthrough success ever. What would that breakthrough success be?

Capture your thoughts on paper. Then, once you have finished the exercise, stay open to ideas and intuitions that will come to you as you go about your day. Then, after three days, reassess your notes and ask yourself the same questions again.

Prepare yourself for some mind-blowing discoveries and turnarounds.

Video Option: J. K. Rowling's Speech "Fringe Benefits of Failure"
Time needed: 21 minutes

Listen to J. K. Rowling's Harvard commencement speech on YouTube titled "The Fringe Benefits of Failure, and the Importance of Imagination." On YouTube, type: "J. K. Rowling Speaks at Harvard Commencement." It's one of the best, funniest, most uplifting, and most inspiring videos about the benefits of failure.

Most people never run far enough on their first wind
to find out they've got a second. Give your dreams all you've
got and you'll be amazed at the energy that comes out of you.
—William James

Points to Remember

Your viewpoint changes everything. Most apparent tragedies are actually blessings in disguise, gift packages that you have to unwrap. Every seeming tragedy or failure will contain in it the seeds of a great victory and success.

If you focus obsessively on opportunities, you can turn any seeming failure around.

Criticism: Heed It or Beat It?

Criticism, even when you try to ignore it, can hurt.
I have cried over many articles written about me,
but I move on and I don't hold on to that.
—Diana Ross

To avoid criticism say nothing, do nothing, be nothing.
—Aristotle

A friend of mine, a prominent employee at one of the giants in Silicon Valley, sounded nervous. He had just published his first book, and we discussed how it had gone.

With big-time endorsements by celebrities, presidents of several countries, dignitaries, Nobel laureates, and CEOs, he had it all. There would be editorials in the *New York Times* and the *International Herald Tribune*. This guy was flying!

But he wasn't talking about that. He said that an article a critic had written about him had left him devastated. It was so negative and unfounded that my friend had taken it as a personal attack.

I laughed and said: "You simply cannot take criticism like that seriously. Some people just want to make you feel bad about what you do, no matter what. This guy probably blamed you for even existing."

But I knew how he felt.

The 13-Year-Old and Rachmaninoff

I was thinking back to when I was 13. I was sitting at the piano in fear, waiting for my teacher to arrive.

She was one of the best teachers around. But she was also one of the harshest critics I was ever to come across. When you are 13 and learning to play one of Rachmaninoff's masterpieces, the Prelude in C Minor, criticism sucks. Not only that, but it hurts and it undermines the very foundation of your motivation and your progress.

She was German. Growing up in Germany, I knew that Germans love to criticize. There is this vague notion that it will somehow make you stronger, bigger, and better if you continue to beat yourself—and others—up.

My piano teacher praised me only once during my many years of studying with her. And when the time came for me to decide whether I wanted to be a professional classical pianist, guess what I said: no. The answer was easy.

In hindsight, it was the right choice because it allowed me to start writing my own music and begin my career as a singer, songwriter, and music producer. But from a larger perspective, even if I had wanted to become a professional classical pianist, she would have drained my last drop of motivation. Who wants to truly dedicate himself to a life of misery?

There Will Always Be Criticism—How You Deal with It Is What's Important

Of course, there are wiser music teachers. One of them is the cellist that professor Jack Canfield wrote about in his Success Principles. She told her students simply not to listen to the critiques in the papers and to shut out criticism altogether.

And she was right.

Don't expect that there will be no criticism when you do what you love. *How* you deal with that criticism is what's important.

Stephen King was chastised by his high school English teacher for his early writing efforts because he wasn't writing about things she felt were appropriate. He later went on to sell more than 300 million books. Stephen says that whenever you try to do something you are passionate about, whether it's writing, singing, or dancing (or starting your own business, I would add), someone else will try to make you feel bad about it.

I know countless examples of employees who had terrific ideas about how to improve products and services that were turned down by their superiors. They were laughed at or told that they were exceeding their authority. One of the reasons why entrepreneurs like Branson are so successful is that they encourage creativity and original, out-of-the-box thinking by their employees. They encourage their employees to try something new, even if it means they screw up.

The Inner Critic

The very first video I showed to the Manchester Business School MBA class was a video titled "Best Motivation Video." Do a search for it on YouTube and take a moment to watch it.

It dismantles the idea that all the great athletes, inventors, businessmen, statesmen, and artists did not receive criticism. They did. Again, it was simply how they dealt with it that made all the difference.

It's an excellent lesson about why not to listen to negative criticism from the outside (or the inside: negative criticism includes that from our own inner critic who constantly puts us down).

Don't even go there. You have to shut this one up completely by not giving it *any* room.

I know people have told you that it works to beat yourself up. It doesn't.

It's like a negativity coach we have hired for ourselves who wants us to cry our heart out and feel miserable because this will magically make us perform better.

When a U.S. talk show host showed Brad Pitt one of the earliest TV ads he had done as a young actor, the audience laughed. It was that bad. Brad just turned around and said: "See, this goes to show you that you can reach anything you put your mind to."

Bang!

When I was a child, my love for music and the piano got on my parents' nerves so much that they finally bought me one.

It's the love you have for what you do and the focus on your goals that will get you from good to great—not negative criticism.

Positive Criticism: The Voice of a Friend

I was having dinner with one of my best friends. We had known each other since university and had been through good and bad times together.

He was angry. He told me that I had taken the wrong path and forgotten about what really mattered to me. He told me that I should follow my heart, my core genius, and devote more time to where my heart was telling me to go.

While his wife was serving her homemade pizzas, I thought about what he had said. I didn't like it because it meant that I had to change my course. At that moment, it was not what I wanted to hear, and I hated him for that. We don't like to change our course.

Many months later, I realized he was right.

When good friends tell you that you've messed up, you'd better listen. That's why they're good friends. That's why you have them. That's what they're there for.

And that's the only type of criticism you should be listening to: that from trusted friends and advisors who point you in the direction of your core genius, the full part of the glass, your talents, the things you do best and love most, your heart's desires.

That's what I mean by messing up: when you have forgotten your own path, started to live someone else's agenda, and urgently need a course correction.

Remember what we talked about in the section on the secret success formula? It's the formula applied by the high achievers and top performers in any field, from business to the creative arts to sports: you have to focus on what you do best and not even look at the other half of the circle, the one that's empty. Jack Canfield called it "your core genius." I like that.

You have to surround yourself with the right people who complement you, make up for what you lack most, and love to do what you hate.

True friends will take you there.

Negative criticism comes from people who do not understand this simple truth about what makes great people great. When you listen to negative criticism, you will begin to focus on the half-empty part of the circle, whether you want to or not.

So don't even go there. Not even for a split second.

The Final Filter

Don't forget: you are your own ultimate and greatest authority. That's your final filter when it comes to criticism: check back with your own inner guidance system.

Here's the sequence:

1. Close the door to negative criticism and shut it tight. This includes criticism from both the inside and the outside.

2. Open the door to criticism from your most trusted friends and advisors who point you into the right direction: the direction of your core genius, the half-full part of the circle.

3. Check the final filter. You are your own ultimate and greatest authority, and so you will have to decide for yourself what to take in and what not.

EXERCISE: The Vow Not to Listen

Time needed: 1 minute

Get in front of a mirror. Yes, a mirror.

Raise your right hand.

Speak after me: "I vow not to listen to any negative criticism *at all*, whether it's from the outside or the inside. I will tell my inner negativity coach to shut up and the people criticizing me on the outside to go away!"

Feels good, doesn't it?

Let's continue: "I further pledge to open the door to the friends and advisors who know me well and have my best interests at heart. I will listen to what they have to say, but I will use my own inner guidance as the final filter. I am my own greatest and ultimate authority."

You have to really do it to feel the effect. You may think it's silly, but the most effective things can seem silly to our well-educated minds. It's silly to use your blow dryer in the bathroom as a mic and sing, yet this is how stars are born.

> Don't pay any attention to what they write
> about you. Just measure it in inches.
> —Andy Warhol

> I have yet to find the man, however exalted his station,
> who did not do better work and put forth greater effort under
> a spirit of approval than under a spirit of criticism.
> —Charles Schwab

Points to Remember

Don't expect that there will be no criticism when you do what you love. How you deal with that criticism is what's important.

There are two forms of criticism: negative criticism and the criticism from trusted friends and advisors who point you in the direction of your core genius and encourage you to follow it. Don't listen to the first, but embrace the latter.

Negative criticism also includes our own inner critic, who constantly puts us down. Don't even go there. You have to shut this one up completely by not giving it *any* room.

In the end, you are your own ultimate and greatest authority. You will have to decide for yourself what to take in and what not.

It's your love for what you do and your focus on your goals that will get you from good to great, not negative criticism.

Change Is Your Friend

> You create your own reality. Remind yourself that you can
> grow into that future (you want to create) as easily as you
> have grown from the past into the present!
> —Jane Roberts

Whatever you want to change, whatever event you want to create, whatever things you want to accomplish: You have to develop a healthy disregard for whatever exists in your life that you do not want to be there. You simply have to choose not to focus on it. This may sound absurd or even foolish in the face of obstacles, but it is the only sane thing to do.

Why? Because these are the images you do not want to focus on; you want to focus on what you want to create or attract. You have to disregard whatever doesn't fit into that picture of yourself or your life. Look at it as if it was a product from your past, created by decisions and mental processes that you chose to engage in for whatever reason. In order to change your life right now, you have to forget about that past, forget about those decisions, and about that part of yourself who created these events or circumstances.

Think of those negative events or circumstances as being a heavy winter coat that you take off as spring approaches. It's become too heavy, too cumbersome. It hinders your movements, so you take it off and put it aside. You shove it away into a remote closet.

One morning you wake up and you have forgotten about it entirely. That's when the magic happens.

Remind yourself that change is the only constant in your life. While most people think of change as an adversary, think of it as a friend. Change will bring you to your new destination as surely as it brought you to where you are today. Think of change as being a river, and your life as being a boat on that river. You're looking out at the changing landscape while the river is slowly taking you to the ocean. You can guide your boat, but you can't guide the direction of the river. You have to trust that it will take you there. Trust the river like a friend; trust change like a friend. As I say in another chapter, embrace change and embrace yourself—what you want and your wishes. Change and your desires go hand in hand. Change will take you to the fulfillment of your desires if you let it.

Let Desire and Passion Fuel Your Journey

Another great line from Jane Roberts's book is, "You get what you focus on." This has obviously been reused countless times in many other books throughout the ages. It's one of those universal principles that I reiterate constantly in many different forms throughout this book.

In the creative arts—as in any other area of life—one of the biggest obstacles is looking at and focusing on your mistakes. Maybe it's easier for a creative artist to not focus on the things we don't want because we are so fueled by passion for what we want to accomplish. We are driven by that inner desire to create something that is of value, to let the inside out, to let our soul speak through art. This is what drives us, motivates us, and makes us get up in the morning. Even if we don't know exactly where we want to go, we know we will get there if we follow that inner passion and desire. This is such a powerful force that it instills in us an insane optimism that could be called downright foolish. It is that vision of accomplishing and creating something extraordinary and great out of nothing that is the basis and the foundation of any great work of art.

In the same way, though, ordinary people accomplish extraordinary things by just following their inner drive and passion.

Why should you care? You can use that to your advantage. Whatever you put your mind to and whatever you fuel by your desire and your passion, you can accomplish. But you have to develop, nurture, support, and reinforce that healthy disregard for what exists in your life right now that you do not want to be there. In musicians' terms, forget those wrong notes and those failed attempts.

Trust in Your Own Way

While I was dealing with skin cancer, one of my biggest objectives was definitely not telling anyone about the diagnosis—keeping it to myself, keeping my mouth shut, and keeping my mind tightly focused on my objective: healing myself. My wife was waiting for me in the car when I came back, and so was another member of my family. I knew that if I told anyone about the diagnosis, they would constantly remind me of my condition (of course with the best intentions!). They would have tried to help me get better. They would have recommended their own way of going about dealing with the problem.

They would have constantly asked about my condition or recommended ways to remedy the situation. In any case, despite their best intentions, all of this would have reinforced my awareness of the condition that I wanted to get rid of. How does this apply to your life? It goes to show that people may have the best intentions and really want to help, but what counts is the way you go about dealing with the problem, the perspective you take, and what you focus on in your thoughts and actions. They have to be totally aligned with your purpose and objective. The more you can align them, the faster you will get there.

Shift Your Focus Away from the Problem

To deal with any problem or circumstance in your life and create a new reality, you have to shift your focus away from whatever it is that you want to change, from the undesired to what it is that you want to create.

Suppose you grew up in humble circumstances in a little town in Australia, but you wanted to become a multimillionaire and enjoy the lifestyle of the rich and famous, with yachts and properties around the globe. Meet my friend Gary Fisher.

As a young man without a big name or cash, Gary set out to create one of the most successful privately owned software companies in the world. Objective is not only one of the mainstream software companies that has outlived 90 percent of computing companies in the last 30 years, but it is also one of the world leaders in enterprise content management. And it's privately owned. How did Gary do it? He ignored all the circumstances that were not in favor of his personal goals, focused steadfastly on his vision, teamed up with the right partners, and put a lot of action behind it. As he says: "You need clarity of vision, you need to know what you want, and you have to put a plan in place to make it happen. You simply cannot focus on obstacles."

Suppose you live in a rural village in Austria and you want to become the best bodybuilder in the world, a world-famous actor, and a successful politician, like Arnold Schwarzenegger. I remember when I first told one of my friends that I wanted to create the World Peace Foundation with the support of Nobel laureates like the Dalai Lama. She laughed in my face. When I told her that I wanted to get a private audience with the Dalai Lama, which only presidents and a handful of other selected individuals around the world ever receive, she laughed even harder. When I showed her the picture of me and the Dalai Lama at my private audience in his hotel suite in Memphis several years later, she didn't laugh anymore.

You can accomplish whatever you set your mind to, but you have to go against the grain of what your friends, family, society, or anybody else may be telling you. Especially if you want to set records in any discipline or do something that no one else has ever done before, you have to develop a healthy disregard for the impossible, and for people telling you "how things are done." Forget 'em!

Develop a Renegade Attitude

Richard Branson certainly has a renegade attitude. He has made a habit of going against whatever any industry he enters into considers a standard. He has developed a healthy disregard for the impossible and the common set of belief systems that is prevalent in society and business. He has applied that mindset to other areas, too, including his numerous record-breaking athletic adventures around the world. What he wants to show us is simply this: you can accomplish whatever you set your mind to—if you go for it, trust and believe in yourself, and then find your own truths and your own way.

Henry Ford was told it couldn't be done when he set out to increase the speed of production of the mass-produced automobile. Dean Kamen, the inventor of the Segway PT (a two-wheeled self-balancing personal transportation device), told his team before inventing his revolutionary electric vehicle: "Listen, I don't care about what anyone else might be saying. The only law that counts for me is Newton's law of gravity and that's it!" So what happened? He set out to do the impossible and succeeded. Now you can even see police forces around the world patrolling on Segways.

All this is true for whatever industry or profession you are in, whatever situation you find yourself in, and whatever your goal or status or finances or experiences or skill sets. Set your goal, go for it, find your own way, and disregard anything else.

EXERCISE: Take Your Mind Off Your Problem to Create a New Reality

Time needed: 2 minutes

Let's put this into practice.

Take any area of your life that you want to change. Take something that's been bugging you, the stone in your shoe. Now take a minute to brainstorm and see how you have been focusing on this—how you've been reinforcing this condition in your daily life and when talking to others.

I want you to recognize your role, or the role you have given to others, in making this condition or circumstance a constant and firm part of your life through your thoughts and actions.

Again, you have been doing all this with the best of intentions. You may want to get rid of the problem, but you've simply chosen the wrong approach.

Now take another minute to close your eyes and brainstorm about how you could go about things differently. How you could actually *not* focus on this condition. How you could respond to others differently. How you could not let others make it such a big part of your life and constantly reinforce that negative condition.

Take a moment to paint a different mental picture of yourself. Imagine yourself with a brush in your hand, a white canvas in front of you, and a palette of a million different colors to create your ideal life. Paint that picture without the stone in your shoe and then see how, even though the stone may still be there, you can actually choose not to focus on it.

I want you to trust and believe that those reactions and that behavior are entirely possible. I want you to affirm to yourself that this is the behavior you will use and this is the behavior that others will display toward you from now on. I want you to constantly reinforce that picture and go back to it as you go about your days.

As a Chinese proverb says: "Only the dead fish swim with the river." Enjoy the ride!

Life is like music, it must be composed by ear,
feeling and instinct, not by rule.
—Paracelsus, Renaissance alchemist

> I don't want to think about how many people
> have thought or still think I'm crazy.
> —Dean Kamen

Points to Remember

Whatever you want to change, whatever event you want to create, whatever goals you want to accomplish, you have to develop a healthy disregard for whatever exists in your life that you do not want to be there. You simply have to choose not to focus on those things. This may sound absurd or even foolish, but it is the only sane thing to do.

To change any problem or circumstance in your life and create a new reality, you have to shift your focus away from whatever you want to change, from the undesired state to what it is that you want to create.

What really counts is the way you go about dealing with the problem, the perspective you take, and what you focus on in your thoughts and actions. They have to be totally aligned with your purpose and objective. The more you can align them, the faster you will get there.

How to Remove Fear from Your Dictionary and Live Life Unconditionally

> It takes courage to grow up and become who you really are.
> —e. e. cummings

> Create your own visual style . . . let it be unique for
> yourself and yet identifiable for others.
> —Orson Welles

I still remember him, tucked away in a corner and rather quiet. He was observing, listening attentively to everything I was saying as I took questions from the core group of 30 students at the reception at Manchester Business School.

But he came back strongly after we all went home. He was the first one to drop me an e-mail, asking very good questions in such a way that you could tell he was thinking things through from all angles. The student, let's call him K, was a bright young man who had a zest for knowledge and a burning desire to find the right answers, the ones that would stick.

In one of his e-mails, he wrote: "When you gave the presentation, you briefly talked about living life unconditionally. I would love to hear more on this aspect."

"Can you describe what you would ideally like to see covered in that chapter?" I asked him.

K wrote: "In short, I would want to know how to live fearlessly and how to remove fear from your dictionary."

He continued: "A lot of people live in fear. This could be fear of rejection, fear of what others think of them, fear of losing, and so on. This makes individuals lose hope and not try to live the life they desire. I see a lot of this even here at business school."

The Golden Shoes

I have a number of distinctive trademarks; one of them is my golden shoes. I have a whole collection of them, mostly Nikes. I wear them everywhere I go—even to the UN.

And I never tie them—ever!

Another trademark is my large collection of shell jewelry, from shell necklaces to bracelets and rings made out of sea snails. I love the sea and surfing so much that I always carry the ocean with me.

I still recall my first meeting with the president of the UN General Assembly. "I love your shells!" was the first thing he exclaimed.

Now, what does that have to do with living life unconditionally and without fear?

It means living as yourself and who you really are in the best and truest way possible. It means not compromising. It means celebrating your unique individuality and flamboyance in whatever way makes you happy and feels right for you.

It means not caring about what others think.

People will respond to you in a different way and with a higher level of energy and commitment once you start being more and more yourself.

The Lady in Red

Here's how one of my Leadership Circle students put this into practice and produced immediate results while still following my advice of taking the smallest step:

Hi Tom,

I just wanted to say thank you for your great advice during the last session of the Leadership Circle. I think you are absolutely right about having your own personality expressed, and not caring about what others think. Also, thanks for answering my questions about what to do if recruiters or companies do not share the same opinion with you during your interviews, and I think you are right again in saying that if they cannot share what you believe, then it is not a company you should work for.

The most useful message I took out of the session is about expressing your own personality during networking events. We had a London networking event last week. I was going to wear a suit like most of my classmates, but I remembered what you said, and instead I wore a black dress and a pair of very nice bright red shoes. During the networking session, I had a lovely chat with a very senior person in finance, and he invited me to go to London to have lunch with him. It was the red shoes that caught his attention, and that is how we started our conversation. So I want to say a big thank you to you, as the advice you gave us is really useful and I have personally experienced its value. I am looking forward to the next session.

Everyone Has a Rock Star Inside
Who Wants to Come Out

Let yourself go. If you want, put on an act. The world is your stage!

Discover yourself and who you really are by living life to the fullest.

Why do you think people like Richard Branson are considered brands in themselves? How do you think Richard Branson made Virgin into one of the top 10 brands in the world?

By living his own unique individuality and true personality, and by not caring about what others might think.

Have fun! Play!

That's the rock star attitude: The world is your stage. Rock it—any moment, any place, any time. Celebrate life and that unique individuality in you that's dying to come out.

An earthquake or natural disaster could blow us all into oblivion tomorrow. Then what? Will you have lived your life to its fullest?

If not, do it now. Go for it *all*. Leave an impression, a mark, a legacy.

It's never too late to take the smallest step.

Live Your Own Unique Individuality

Growing up, I was taught to conform, and it didn't serve me well.

I have since learned to live with my own unique energy and flamboyance. That includes my shell jewelry, the infamous golden shoes, lots of pearls, and a dress code that's over the top. As a result, not only do people recognize me instantly, but it also pushes the boundaries of everything else I'm doing. Since it's not fake but simply who I am, it's a natural expression of myself. Therefore, it helps me to act boldly on my impulses in all other areas of my life.

In order to remove fear from your dictionary, you have to embrace the *bigger you*. Start to act as if you already are who and what you want to become, and the world will change with you.

People will respond to you differently, and unforeseen opportunities will arise. And people will naturally respond to you with more commitments.

On top, you will be rewarded with a ball of fun in the process!

Fear Comes from Not Being in Tune with Yourself

You will never do anything in this world without courage.
It is the greatest quality of the mind next to honor.
—Aristotle

> The more you like yourself, the less you are like
> anyone else, which makes you unique.
> —Walt Disney

Someone once said: the only natural fears we are born with are the fears of falling and of loud noises. All other fears are culturally acquired.

When I first stepped in front of the MBA class at Manchester Business School, I was facing one of the cleverest and most intelligent groups of individuals from around the world—but also one of the most fearful. A big lack of self-confidence and trust pervaded the whole room.

Fear comes from not being in tune with yourself.

K, the student I mentioned earlier, went on to say: "Things that might be specific to a particular group or geography: Individuals add barriers under the label of cultural norms, social beliefs, and so on. For example, there are a lot of families where love marriage is just not an option and people don't marry the person of their choice. These examples are endless, and ideally I would like to see information that allows people to break free of patterns and other false beliefs." Good point.

I'm in no position to judge cultural norms. But I promise you this: you simply can't deny love in such an important part of your life as your personal relationships and then expect to excel in your professional life doing what you love.

It just doesn't work that way. You can't have your cake and eat it, too. If you severely hamper yourself in one area, you will affect all the other areas of your life.

When you put a damper on something as important as your relationship or whom you ought to marry, it will affect each and every area of your life.

The reverse is also true. If you free yourself, even a tiny bit, from the old barriers, patterns, false beliefs, and limits you have put on yourself, you will feel liberated and have more energy in all areas of your life.

That's why I recommend again and again that you should take the smallest step in the right direction—it will immediately free you.

You can't expect to have loads of fun in business, push the boundaries, and have a ball of fun doing what you love if you severely limit yourself and are afraid to follow your own natural energy and leanings.

Don't sacrifice. Don't compromise.

Anyone Can Be Flamboyant

I asked K what else he would like to see covered in this chapter besides what I have written already.

He said: "When you talk about yourself or you give examples of people like Richard Branson, people will say: 'Well, Tom's got such an awesome worldwide network of people already, of course he can dress in whatever way he wants, do what he likes and not need to conform. He gets away with it. And Richard Branson is super famous and a billionaire; of course he can do whatever he likes and not care.'"

I understand that it might look that way. But it's actually the other way around.

I didn't know anybody when I started to build up my whole network from scratch. I wasn't born with a silver spoon in my mouth, and I didn't have a big name.

As my friend Chade-Meng Tan, Google's former head of personal growth and author of the *New York Times* bestseller *Search Inside Yourself*, says: "My dear friend Tom Oliver is an inspiring example that a person in ordinary circumstances with the right intention can accomplish extraordinary things."

I'm giving you advice on how to accomplish extraordinary things and have a ball of fun doing it—by trusting yourself, and by being who you really are.

Whatever your circumstances, the principles are always the same: be yourself and live your own unique individuality in whatever way this translates to your personal or professional life.

Don't imitate. Use other people's examples to inspire you to find your own way and discover what works best for *you*.

Sara Blakely used the Richard Branson rock star business attitude to create a billion-dollar company, Spanx, with $5,000—and she owns it all.

Branson was able to create his brand by being a rebel, by constantly reinventing himself and ignoring what other people told him couldn't be done. That's why he called the company Virgin: every new market he enters, he has no prior experience in. That allows him to approach it with a beginner's mind and rethink the industry's processes from top to bottom.

He didn't start as a household name and he wasn't born with a silver spoon in his mouth, either. Richard's stunts, like jumping from buildings, going around the planet in a balloon, and doing crazy kite-surfing moves, have been among the key elements in turning Virgin into the top brand it is today.

EXERCISE: Wake Up to Your Own Unique Individuality

Time needed: 3 minutes

Reread the story from my Leadership Circle student and see how you could translate this to your personal or professional life in whatever way suits you best. Let it inspire you to take the smallest step toward living as the *true you* with your unique individuality. This works whether you are a student going for a job interview or a CEO going into his next board meeting.

Ask yourself: what would be the smallest step I could take *right now* to not care and get rid of my fears?

Whether it means dressing a bit more flashily or wearing those golden sneakers or buying that pair of pink headphones, I don't care. Whatever works for you works for me.

Don't be fooled by flashy cars, big paychecks, or fancy suits; the people at the top often conform just as much as the guys at the bottom of the food chain. It's a fear of not fitting in—a fear that we cannot be ourselves and still be wildly successful.

Trust me: you can.

Start small and wear those red shoes to your next meeting. You might be just as surprised by the results!

There is a vitality, a life force, an energy, a quickening,
that is translated through you into action, and because
there is only one of you in all time, this expression is unique.
—Martha Graham

I learned that courage was not the absence of fear, but
the triumph over it. The brave man is not he who does
not feel afraid, but he who conquers that fear.
—Nelson Mandela

Points to Remember

In order to remove fear from your dictionary, you have to embrace the *bigger you*. Start to act as if you already are who and what you want to become, and the world will change with you.

I'm giving you advice on how to accomplish extraordinary things and have a ball of fun doing it—by trusting yourself, and by being who you really are. People will respond to you differently and with more commitments. Unforeseen opportunities will arise.

You simply can't deny love in such an important part of your life as your personal relationships and then expect to excel in your professional life doing what you love. Fear comes from not being in tune with yourself. If you free yourself, even a tiny bit, from the old barriers, patterns, false beliefs, and limits you have put on yourself, you will feel liberated and have more energy in all areas of your life.

Whatever your circumstances, the principles are always the same: be yourself in whatever way this translates to your personal or professional life. Let it inspire you to take even the smallest step toward living as the *true you* with your own unique individuality.

Don't imitate. Use other people's examples to inspire you to find your own way and discover what works best for *you*.

Step 7

Cooperate for Success

Life Is Based on Cooperation

Competition has been shown to be useful up
to a certain point and no further, but cooperation,
which is the thing we must strive for today,
begins where competition leaves off.
—Franklin D. Roosevelt

When I went to the Wharton School of Business and Finance at the University of Pennsylvania, our favorite Christmas present for our parents was a T-shirt that had two businessmen on it. They were shaking hands to seal a business deal and smiling at each other, but behind their backs, they were holding a knife and a baseball bat in the other hand. It made our parents laugh. However, it also showed the problematic ethical foundation in the financial industry, which ultimately led to the global financial crisis many years later.

We Have to Learn to Cooperate to an Unprecedented Degree

Most of the challenges we are facing today are global: climate change, lack of fresh water, overpopulation, conflict over scarce resources, growing socioeconomic inequality, and the marginalization of millions of people. Add to this the lack of purpose and fulfillment on a personal level that millions are facing every day. Most of these global challenges we are facing today stem from the belief that life is based on cutthroat competition, not cooperation. Nothing could be further from the truth. Life is based on cooperation. And to solve these global challenges, individuals and businesses alike will have to learn to cooperate to an unprecedented degree.

Cooperation Leads to the Best Results

When I went to Wharton, we were graded on the bell curve, which meant that we were always competing against one another. This instilled the kind of cutthroat competition that made it impossible to ask anyone to share his or her notes if you missed a class. However, it´s cooperation that produces the best results. The individuals, businesses, and global brands that are now learning to cooperate will be the ones that will come out on top in the future.

I often integrate live music performances into my speeches and keynotes and have the audience sing along with me while I am playing the piano. Why? Because as we sing, we suddenly move and feel as one. There is no more separation. I have done this with all kinds of different audiences, from business school students to elite groups of world-class artists, heads of state, billionaires, and CEOs. The results are always astounding. Afterward, I ask everyone to try to capture that feeling of oneness and cooperation they felt when we were singing together in harmony and to apply it to everything else they are doing in business and in life. And I promise them that they will get much better results!

The Magic Thread

As a live performer, singer, and songwriter I have had the pleasure of experiencing what it's like to make music in a band. When you are playing together and performing on stage, there is no way you can do this in a competitive way. There is an invisible harmony among all the band members. It is as if a magic thread united everyone in the group so that the band members know and feel one another's movements before they are even made. They move as one. This is how the whole band can improvise on the spot and react to sudden changes in the music. There is a beauty and a magic to this that anyone, and especially businesses, can learn a lot from.

To quote my friend Jez Frampton, Global Group CEO of Interbrand, "Businesses don't jam enough to ensure their long-term success."

Oneness

As you know by now, I love to surf. As a surfer, you are very much in harmony with the ocean and the planet. When you are surfing, the ocean becomes your office, and you can't really separate yourself from the life "out there." Whenever you are surfing, there comes a magical moment when you feel "all one" with nature and the world surrounding you. There is no more separation. Afterward, you come back to your own life and business with a new sense of harmony, oneness, and cooperation. And, of course, you achieve much better results. Try to experience a similar feeling of oneness whenever you can, and I promise you the results will be astounding.

EXERCISE: The Magic Thread

Time needed: 2 minutes

Remember the last time you felt a true sense of cooperation when you were completing a group task or project, even if it was with just one other person, and even if it wasn't part of your professional life, but rather a fun project or hobby. Ask yourself: What were the results? Was it effortless compared to some other projects that were based on a sense of cutthroat competition? Was it fun?

After thinking back to this episode for two minutes, try to capture that feeling of cooperation. As in the example of my playing the piano and everyone singing during my keynotes, try to apply this sense of cooperation to everything else you are doing, in business and in life. And be assured: you will get much better results. On top of that, it will be a lot more fun.

No employer today is independent of those
about him. He cannot succeed alone, no matter how
great his ability or capital. Business today is more
than ever a question of cooperation.
—Orison Swett Marden

Points to Remember

Life is based on cooperation. To solve the global challenges we are
facing today, individuals and businesses alike have to learn to cooperate to an unprecedented degree. The ones that are now learning to
cooperate will be the ones that will come out on top in the future.
Cooperation always produces the best results. Try to learn from experiences where you felt a true sense of cooperation and apply this sense
to everything else you are doing, in business and in life.

Peace—The Undervalued Currency in Business and Life

If we have no peace, it is because we have
forgotten that we belong to each other.
—Mother Teresa

Peace is its own reward.
—Mahatma Gandhi

The future of any company lies in its ability to attract the top people
as employees. They are the basis for any business of any size, even
the best global brands, to consistently outperform the competition. But
now more than ever, the top people are not attracted by the best pay
alone. They want to work with the best global corporate citizens.

What does it mean to be a good global corporate citizen? It means
to be at peace with your world. This is based on a concept of inner
and outer peace that includes the external corporate behavior but also
peace within the company. Consequently, to be a good corporate citizen

means to build a better company and thereby ensure its long-term success. Otherwise the employees will route a company out and then ultimately its customers as well. Rising expectations of the millennial generation intensifies the need for corporations to become better global corporate citizens, living up to the highest ethical standards.

Peace Leads to Higher Levels of Creativity, Innovation, and Much Better Results

To turn any business into a true global corporate citizen—a place to which high achievers and top talent naturally gravitate—you have to integrate peace into the company's internal corporate code. This is true if you are an entrepreneur, team leader, or running a billion-dollar enterprise. It doesn't matter if your team is composed of two people or forty thousand. You have to solidly incorporate this concept of peace into your leadership style so that your team can thrive and you can produce the best results.

To create peace within an organization is a secret ingredient that's unfortunately often overlooked or undervalued. To reduce conflict within an organization and to promote harmony ultimately produces more cooperation between the different groups within the organization and different team members within a project. This in turn creates a higher sense of creativity and innovation and thereby produces much better results.

Integrate Peace into Your Leadership Style

It is surprising to me how much energy is wasted even in large corporations on internal conflicts. This energy should much rather be spent on preventing and reducing conflicts. Much to my surprise, conflict resolution and prevention are not taught at most schools around the world, not even at universities, let alone business schools. So it's no wonder it hasn't really entered the corporate boardroom or culture. In the same way that these concepts should ideally be part of every course curriculum, tools to prevent and reduce conflict should be an integral part of a company's DNA and executive leadership and training programs. If you can integrate the concept of peace into your leadership style, you can be sure that you will be able to attract the best people and top talent for your projects or business.

EXERCISE: Become Your Own Buddha in Business
Time needed: 5 minutes

Inner peace is a habit you can cultivate, but you have to very actively pursue it and make it a regular part of your day.

Take a sheet of paper and write "Inner peace is key to my success" at the top. Then make a list of activities that you've come across in your life that give you a sense of that inner peace. List everything, no matter how small or trivial it may sound. Even if it is an activity that may seem silly to you but it does give you that sense of inner peace, put it down. After five minutes take a good look at that list, take a step back, and ask yourself: "What could I put into practice—right here, right now—that would give me a sense of inner peace and take the least amount of time and resources?" Then schedule an appointment with yourself, ideally once a day, to make that quality a firm part of your life.

Peace begins with a smile.
—Mother Teresa

Points to Remember

To turn any business into a true global corporate citizen—a place to which high achievers and top talent naturally gravitate—you have to integrate peace into the company's internal corporate code.

To reduce conflict within an organization and to promote harmony ultimately produces more cooperation between the different groups within the organization and different team members within a project. This creates a higher sense of creativity and innovation and thereby leads to much better results.

If you can integrate the concept of peace within your organization into your leadership style, you can be sure that you will be able to attract the best people and top talent for your projects or business.

Happiness in 15 Minutes

I slept and I dreamed that life is all joy. I woke and I saw that
life is all service. I served and I saw that service is joy.
—Khalil Gibran, *The Prophet*

Every man must decide whether he will walk in the light of
creative altruism or in the darkness of destructive selfishness.
—Martin Luther King, Jr.

Some years ago, I went out to do some late-night grocery shopping and saw an old homeless man going through the trash cans behind our house.

I went past him and suddenly took a deep look in his eyes.

Then something astounding happened: I realized that it was me that I was looking at. Not on an intellectual, but on a deep emotional level, I realized that this could have been *me*—an older version of myself, but me. This is when *Ubuntu* hit me—Desmond Tutu often refers to this African saying, which means: "I am because *you are*."

It shocked me.

Worries were swept away, and the little things I had been preoccupied with before I left the house were gone. All I could think of was helping this man.

I went right back to our apartment, told my wife what had happened, and went through our place in a wild rush to get my hands on anything that could help him before he was gone.

We took blankets, food, and sodas. We hurried downstairs and found him a few hundred feet away looking through other trash cans. We went up to him and gave him what we had, then we both went to an ATM and withdrew money. We were lucky; he was still in our street. We went up to him and gave him the money. The deep feeling of gratitude in his eyes and his smile have stayed with me to this day.

When I later saw him approach a pizza place and order a pizza with some of the money we had given him, I had tears in my eyes. He held the note in his hand with the posture of pride and joy that someone who usually had to search through the trash for leftovers could have.

Helping Others Makes You Happy and Creates a Life of Abundance

Fast-forward to today.

Besides having founded one of the most respected and influential peace charities in the world, the World Peace Festival and World Peace Foundation, which Desmond Tutu, recipient of the Nobel Peace Prize, has called "the most influential peace gathering in history," I have made helping homeless people in our city, together with my wife, a weekly ritual.

We recently bought pizzas for a whole group of homeless people who slept in a public place right next to the Nice harbor, a stone's throw from where some of the biggest yachts in the world are anchored, some of them worth $30 million or more.

I approached them, introduced myself, and then asked each one what his favorite pizza topping was. Some answered directly and with confidence. Others were amazed and had to pause for a moment. They were no longer used to being asked what their favorite was—in anything.

When I handed them the stack of pizzas half an hour later, they all introduced themselves to me and gave me a hug. When I joined their group and sat down with them, one of them asked: "Why are you doing this?"

And I replied, "Because it makes me happy."

This is why the Dalai Lama smiled when he told me in a private audience: "Altruism is the biggest egoism." He's a very smart man.

Altruism is the biggest egoism because it instantly puts a smile on your face and creates more happiness in your life.

Something amazing happens: suddenly your worries are swept away and you feel overwhelmed by joy, love, and gratitude.

EXERCISE: Reach Out

Time needed: 15 minutes, and then a lifetime

It doesn't matter whether you are rich or poor. A dollar can help someone who is homeless to see another day.

And help doesn't come in the form of money alone: ask one of your friends or family members who is truly in need how you can help.

Give so that it stretches you a little. The goal is not to make you feel aloof or proud, but to put that wide smile on your face.

> Do your little bit of good where you are; it's those little
> bits of good put together that overwhelm the world.
> —Desmond Tutu

Points to Remember

Altruism is the biggest egoism because it truly makes you happy and brings more abundance into your life. Do whatever you can to help and reach out, on a local or, if possible, global scale.

To give unconditionally unlocks immense powers. It makes you value what you have, makes you feel grateful for what's good in your life, makes you focus on the half-full part of the glass, and unlocks hidden opportunities that you weren't even aware of. This is why, ultimately, it creates more abundance—in all areas of your life.

How to Create a Worldwide Network from Scratch, with No Big Name and No Cash

> Vision is the art of seeing what's invisible to others.
> —Jonathan Swift

This is definitely one of the top 10 questions I'm asked most often, whether by people who are just starting out or by others who already have a great network in place: "How did you create a worldwide, first-class network from scratch with no big name and no cash?"

As I've said before, I wasn't born with a silver spoon in my mouth. I didn't have a trust fund, either. And I certainly didn't have a big name.

You might think that creating a network is easier if you are born with a big name because it will open doors. That's true, but then again, it will not keep you in the room. Not being born with a great name also has an upside: it means that you have no baggage. You can write your own story.

The cash is the other element. "I/We don't have enough cash" is the number one excuse that kills thousands of great projects before they even start. And it's not so much an excuse as a misunderstanding. You will see that, now more than ever before, you don't need to have a lot of cash in order to create a worldwide, high-caliber network from scratch—even one that's totally over the top. This applies equally to any individual, start-up, team, medium-sized company, or even global conglomerate.

Let me share some of the secrets of how to create a "Lamborghini of networks," as one of my PAs called it. It's always the same three-step process.

Step 1: Define Your Big Vision—This Is Your Big Name!

Whether you are in Detroit or in a small town in Arkansas, or in Mumbai, Beijing, or Berlin, you've got to have a vision that's so compelling that people catch fire.

Then you have to be able to sell that vision very actively and convey it to others with enough passion so that it becomes contagious. This is key.

Passion always wins over numbers, charts, or PowerPoints.

When I started to create the World Peace Foundation, I had a very clear vision of what I wanted to accomplish. In the same way, when I'm sitting down at the piano and composing a song, I have a clear inner vision that I try to get across. The more I focus on that vision, the easier it will be to actually get the notes down on paper. Then the music, the melody, and the lyrics will form by themselves.

The same is true for creating a following for any organization, brand, product, or service.

The clearer your vision, the easier it will be for you to actually pull it off and convince others to follow.

How does that operate in businesses or multinational corporations?

A lot of big corporations face challenges when it comes to inspiring their top-level management and employees to buy into the company's vision, especially when the company's strategy changes. Motivating employees in such a way that they begin to live the company's vision on an everyday basis is key to getting consumers engaged and gaining new markets.

Step 2: Fuel Your Vision with Passion—This Is Your Cash

Your passion is your cash!

Not having a lot of cash means that you've got to have another currency that works and that people will respond to. Your passion is that currency.

It's the wings on which you fly. Your passion, if it's honestly felt, will become contagious, and other people will catch fire and will respond to you—with commitments, help, support, and, yes, cash.

This also applies to a corporation that is trying to sell a new product or service. Talk about passion.

Check out the endless queues of people lining up in front of the Apple stores before the launch of a new product. Some even camp out the night before. Just like a rock star, Steve Jobs was able to imbue Apple products with vision, passion, and life.

I often get approached by individuals or corporations who complain that they are fueled by passion but do not have enough resources. I disagree. Passion is the best currency you could have. This is what people (and clients and customers) will ultimately respond to.

Do you really think resources are the most important thing? You could throw literally hundreds of millions of dollars at a new product, service, company, or idea and end up in quicksand. Just look at the millions of dollars that even corporate giants like Google invest in new projects that end up being miserable failures. This happens because the vision wasn't defined clearly enough or the people in charge didn't identify with the actual product they were selling.

Your heart and your soul have to be in it.

Marketing strategies designed by clever individuals with great degrees often lack the most important ingredient that any good salesperson needs to have: passion for the product or service. Often chief marketing officers, board members, or salespeople are so emotionally detached from their own brand, products, or services that it's no wonder these things don't sell.

If you are the CEO of a company that's facing a similar problem, you've got to make heads roll or take a deep look at why your people do not identify with what your company is all about. This will also be a good time to ask yourself the Steve Jobs question: "Do I really want to be doing what I'm doing right now, do I want to continue what I am doing, or is there anything that I would change?"

You'd better create the kind of products and services that truly inspire passion in yourself and in your staff because this will come across to consumers.

Can I Train Passion?

This is a good question that was asked by an entrepreneur from South America in a workshop by Pepsi that I gave. There are two ways to go about it.

Number one: take a look at creative artists and the way a musician prepares for a concert. Artists are by nature passionate and genuine about what they are doing, and these qualities are communicated to band members and audiences. They have to create a vision and imbue it with enough energy and life to excite their audiences.

Check out a live performance of your favorite artist on YouTube and see how he or she excites the audience, the passion that he or she has to get across when performing, and how that is communicated to the crowd.

The way a musician composes a song, prepares for a concert, and then communicates that inner vision to his audiences can be transferred point by point to the corporate world. The bigger and stronger the passion, the easier it is to excite your audience.

Try to emulate that. As a CEO or project leader, you have to develop a vision that's compelling enough to drive your team or your top people. Only then will that vision be communicated to customers and gain its own momentum. Corporations can learn a lot from this in order to motivate their employees and consumers even more effectively.

Number two: the more clearly you define your vision, the stronger your passion will be.

Even though this is almost common sense, few of us follow it. Certainly very few corporations do. But then again, look at the ones that come out on top, both individuals and corporations. You will find that they always have a crystal-clear vision defined on paper.

Muddy vision means muddy passion.

Step 3: Reach Out to the First Person—Keep Your Vision High and the Steps Small

Whether you want to be or not, we are all in sales—*all* the time.

You were already in sales when you were eight and negotiating a pocket money increase with your mom. Whether you are going for a job interview, are selling Tupperware out of your own home, are creating a worldwide movement, are pitching to a client, or are a CEO who's trying to sell his company, you're in sales.

People often ask me how to get to the *right* contacts. That's the wrong question. The process is simple: start with *one* person. Again and again, I keep telling you that you have to start small.

People tend to overcomplicate things.

Start with the first person who comes to mind. It doesn't matter who. Most people place the bar way too high and think endlessly about the right approach and the right first person to contact.

You cannot plan exactly how your network will develop. Instead, focus on gaining *momentum*.

What you *can* plan, though, are the three simple steps given here: concentrate on defining the clear vision of what you want to accomplish, fuel your passion, then go out and create a network of supporters for it.

Most people never pick up the phone because they make things too complicated and place the bar too high. Place the bar as low as possible, take the smallest step, and call somebody. It literally doesn't matter who; just get the ball rolling and get your vision across. You will naturally see and feel who will be committed and who will not, who will respond to you and who will not, and consequently, who will deliver and who won't.

Should I Focus on Creating a Mastermind Group?

> There is no passion to be found playing small—in settling for
> a life that is less than the one you are capable of living.
> —Nelson Mandela

This was a good question from one of my students. A few books recommend creating such a group to help you profit from other people's ideas, advice, and feedback.

The answer is, I'm not a big fan of spending a lot of time on creating a mastermind group. Why? Simply because, most of the time and with most of the people I know, this group will develop naturally out of your network of supporters. So the previous three steps are enough.

This is where I want you to focus your time and energy.

My Story: How I Started

Let me give you an example. One of the very first people I got on board when I was building the worldwide network for my World Peace Foundation was a former professor in California. I got on a plane to visit him simply on a leap of faith. It just felt right. After all, I had to start with somebody somewhere.

He was the first person who came to mind. We had met in a workshop on the Big Island of Hawaii some years before, and I just gave him a call. Of course, you've got to have the cash to get on a plane. But even without it, you could get on a Skype video call instead, and it wouldn't cost you a dime.

When I told him my vision in colorful detail, he immediately caught fire. He started to brainstorm about whom he could reach out to in order to help me make my vision become reality. After an hour or two, we were already on the phone with the president of one of the most famous foundations in the world. He then kept on adding names to the list.

Afterward, I just went from one contact to the next. This simple process has a powerful multiplying effect. As soon as people catch fire, they start connecting you to others, so your tree grows branches. These branches grow additional branches, and so forth. You get the idea. Before you realize it, the growth becomes an avalanche, and your momentum is unstoppable. This is how you create great networks.

In hindsight, almost my *whole* network can be traced back to this single meeting in California.

It helped that, as an artist, I am passionate by nature. This is why it was easy for me to get my vision across with the right level of energy to create momentum. But, as I explained earlier, anybody can learn how to be passionate.

So starting with one person is really all it takes.

You cannot plan a network, but what you *can* plan are the three simple steps given here. And be assured: they will lead to extraordinary results.

EXERCISE: Turbocharge Your Own Network

Time needed: 5 minutes

Think of people you know whom you could tell about your vision and what you want to accomplish. Take five minutes to make a list of 10 to 20 contacts that come to mind easily.

Then circle one name on that list. Schedule a time in your calendar when you will contact that person by phone, by e-mail, or in a personal meeting. (I'm a big fan of face-to-face meetings because they are best at getting your energy across.)

It's as simple as that.

What If I Am a CEO? Same Thing: Start Small and Test!

If you're the CEO of a big corporation, your situation might look slightly different, so here are the steps.

After you have defined your vision clearly enough, make a list of the key influencers and opinion leaders you would like to get on board for your product, service, or brand.

I wouldn't devise any superclever plans, but rather go for the first test subject and start to get momentum. If you have enough resources, of course, you can put 10, 20, 100, or 1,000 people on the list of people you want to get on board. That's fine. But you should first field-test your vision to see where it gets the most traction. Otherwise, you might waste valuable time or resources on elaborate campaigns that produce virtually no results.

I'm always astounded by how much money big corporations spend on campaigns that produce no concrete outcomes because they didn't field-test enough. Somebody somewhere had a great idea, but people lost themselves in PowerPoint charts. It's incredible!

What If I Cannot Get to the People on My List?

This came from one of my students again. It was a misunderstanding, really. I don't want you to reach out to the people you don't know yet; start with the people you *know already*.

It's fine to make a separate list of high-flying supporters you want to get on board, but concentrate on where you are *right now*. Look at my example: almost all of my network started with a single person—and that was someone I knew.

So don't make things too complicated. It's often an excuse not to get started because you might be too afraid of rejection.

> F... it! If that first person doesn't respond to your vision,
> the next one will! You're in sales, get over it!
> —Anonymous

Points to Remember

Your vision is your big name. Your passion is your cash.

You've got to have a vision that's so compelling that people catch fire. Then you have to be able to sell that vision very actively and convey it to others with enough passion so that it becomes contagious. Passion *always* wins over numbers, charts, or PowerPoints.

Concentrate on defining the clear vision of what you want to accomplish, fuel your passion, then go out and create a network of supporters for it.

Most people never pick up the phone because they make things too complicated and place the bar too high. Place the bar as low as possible, take the smallest step, and call somebody. It literally doesn't matter who; get the ball rolling and get your vision across. Starting with one person is really all it takes.

You cannot plan exactly how your network will develop. Instead, focus on gaining *momentum*.

Go from one contact to the next. This simple process has a powerful multiplying effect. As soon as people catch fire, they start connecting you to others, so your tree grows branches. These branches grow additional branches and so forth. Before you realize it, the growth becomes an avalanche, and your momentum is unstoppable. This is how you create great networks.

How to Find the Ideal Partners in Business and in Life: Never Settle for Second Best

If your emotional abilities aren't in hand, if you don't
have self-awareness, if you are not able to manage your
distressing emotions, if you can't have effective relationships,
then no matter how smart you are, you are not going to get very far.
—Daniel Goleman, *Emotional Intelligence*

If you like a person you say "let's go into business together." Man is
a social animal after all, but such partnerships are fraught with danger.
—Brian Tracy

The Most Important Question of All: Are the Visions Aligned?

The question, "Are the visions aligned?" is the most important one in both personal and business relationships. It is surprising to me how often people forget this. It's probably because most of us naturally like to bond, the "social animal" factor that Brian Tracy cites. But it still puzzles me. And I'm no exception! I love people. I love talking to people, and I love doing exciting projects with them. But sometimes I forget the most obvious question: are the visions aligned?

I've just had another situation in which I let one of my business partners go after a year of stress, fatigue, and mediocre results in the partnership because our visions clearly weren't aligned. Did I check them before? No. I was so excited about working with this person because I liked him so much.

Liking someone is fine, but it's a test. If you like hanging out with someone, have a beer with him. It doesn't mean that he's a great partner for a business or for any of your projects.

What's Your Number? The Ideal Partner to Spend Your Life With

Most of us settle. I have no idea why.

I've certainly done my fair share of settling as well. One exercise I came up with to help some of my friends has since worked wonders for many. It introduces math into an otherwise very emotional equation.

Here's a numbers game: as of 2012, there are approximately 7 billion people in the world, and counting. . . .

Out of these 7 billion, guess how many women or men there are in the world, depending on your sexual preference. This is not a math test, so just take a guess.

The final question: out of that pool of eligible partners, with how many could you have a happy and fulfilling relationship with ease? I have heard anything from 10,000 to 100,000 to 1 million. Almost everyone comes up with a different number, and that's OK.

Whatever your number is, that's fine. The whole purpose is to help you break free from mental limitations and therefore prepare you to draw the ideal partner into your life.

The lesson is, there is no *the one*. When I hear people say, "I'm looking for the *one*," they are usually still looking the next time we meet. The truth is, there are about as many *ones* for you in the world as the number you came up with.

Whatever that number is, it will definitely do one thing: free you from the feeling that there is an urgent need for you to settle. You have no reason at all to settle.

Tune In to Your Ideal Partner

> I'm going to be alone. I have no luck with relationships.
> —Halle Berry

When you tune in to your ideal partner, your subconscious mind (and the universe) will be at work day and night to find the right partner for you. Again, don't settle! Once you settle, a mechanism comes into play that the founder of the Silva Method, José Silva, described well: it's as if you are sitting in a restaurant placing your order. Your waiter goes into the kitchen, and the chef gets busy. But then you look at the menu again and decide on another dish. This means that you settle for less, that is, you give an order to the universe and your subconscious that you no longer want an ideal partner, but second best will do just fine.

Then the waiter goes into the kitchen and changes the order. Again, the chef gets busy. Then you look at the menu again. The problem is: if you had had the patience to wait just a little longer after your first order, the waiter would have brought your ideal meal right out. But you changed your mind and your intention.

Some people can live like that all their lives and wonder why they're just not lucky in finding the ideal partner, even though they might be as beautiful, sexy, and successful as Halle Berry!

The lesson is, you can find the ideal partner only if you don't settle. This applies to any relationship or partnership, personal or business.

People can find you only when you tune in to the desire to find the ideal partner and believe that he or she exists. Otherwise, this person might be just around the corner, but you're blocking the opportunity because you are still locked into existing relationships, mentally and physically.

Find Your Ideal Partner in Business

> I always knew I was going to be rich. I never
> doubted it for even a minute!
> —Warren Buffett

It might be more obvious that the big life visions have to be aligned in personal relationships, but this is true for professional relationships and success in business as well. Two people might have completely different characters or personalities but make excellent business partners if their visions are aligned.

Meet the Samwer brothers: Marc, Oliver, and Alexander. Most brothers would dread the idea of ever going into business together. In fact, most coaches and advisors would warn that a triple partnership composed of three brothers is doomed to fail. On top of it, Marc, Oliver, and Alex couldn't be more different from one another.

Marc is the entrepreneurial go-getter type. His eyes always fixed on the big picture, and he will stop at nothing to get a job done and accomplish his goals. This even shows up in details such as his desk, which is always neatly organized and spotless so that he never loses sight of the big picture. He's got the drive of a bulldozer and the tenacity of a pit bull. If Marc is set on "go," nothing can stop him. At the same time, he's very likable and a great people person.

Oliver is smart and financially astute. He's also a very gifted strategic thinker. While he might not be the ideal type for the front line or to win the hearts and minds of potential investors or clients over a beer, he is very adept at playing a strategic role behind the scenes.

Alexander, the youngest, was among the best in his graduating class in all of Germany. He's probably the most intelligent of the three, and I would call him the engineer in this trio. He brings a keen eye and attention to detail that the others might miss. His personality is rather shy and reserved.

I still remember sitting with them in the living room of their parents' house when Marc and I were just 17. We were good friends, and we had just started a debating club in our local high school. Even at the tender ages of 18, 17, and 16, the hearts and minds of the three brothers were dead set on a common goal, and their visions were aligned. The one thing they kept talking about was their goal of going into business together. It wasn't just a family bond—they shared exactly the same vision. This was their ultimate goal for the rest of their lives. It created a powerful force that turned them into an unbeatable power trio.

They had a clear plan, too: they would all study different subjects and finish their university degrees first, and then go on to accomplish great things together. They did not doubt for even a minute that their vision would be a success.

In fact, their personal visions were so aligned and so strong that their mother quit her well-paid job at one of the largest insurance companies in the world after Alexander finished high school because she felt that her sons were destined to succeed in a big way. She wanted to do everything she could to nurture and support their vision.

It didn't take long for their success to show.

Right before the dot-com boom, Oliver interviewed the CEOs of the most promising Silicon Valley firms for his university thesis in management. Behind this was a clear plan: to copy the best and most profitable U.S. Internet startup and create a similar one in Europe at a time when the Internet craze was just in its infancy. Their plan was to go for as much market share as possible and then be bought by the U.S. company that was the model for their European copy. They chose to model their company after eBay and called it Alando.

Three months after they started, eBay bought their start-up for almost $100 million, a record at the time—not bad pay for three months of work. They were made head of eBay Europe and were responsible for the rapid foreign expansion of the U.S. giant. But they didn't stop there. After leaving eBay, the Samwer brothers continued to create a wide range of start-ups and Internet ventures in a variety of different industries, from mobile communications to social networks. Today they have a combined net worth of more than a billion dollars and were among the few private investors who held a personal stake in Facebook before it went public.

This shows that if your visions are aligned, the power of a partnership is unstoppable. There's no limit to what you can accomplish.

Whenever you enter into a partnership where the partners' visions and intentions are not aligned, you immediately set yourself up for failure, a lot of friction, stress, and poor or at best mediocre results. This is true for both personal and professional partnerships.

EXERCISE: Align the Visions—Professional Partnerships

Time needed: 15 to 30 minutes

Go back to the example of Marc and his brothers, and do the same with whoever is your partner on a professional basis. I have seen people ask the question "Where do you ideally see yourself in a few years' time?" within the first 10 or 15 minutes of a conversation.

This is not meant to be an indiscretion. Checking whether or not your visions are aligned is usually a sign of a very high-caliber and experienced professional who doesn't want to waste his or your time.

The final step is to compare the visions. Be honest. Trust me, this takes guts, both in business and in life. But it's absolutely necessary, and it's the most overlooked item bar none for success in the business world.

This is true as well if you are going for a merger. Align the visions of the corporate partners in the prospective merger and save yourself a lot of stress and dinero later.

EXERCISE: Align the Visions—Personal Partnerships
Time needed: 15 to 30 minutes

But personal relationships are a toughie. We are so in love or so taken by someone's personality, appearance, intelligence, or whatever that we switch off our brains. While this is OK and necessary to some extent, we should nevertheless not forget the moment of truth when we arrive at the point where we are seriously considering settling down with somebody.

I know a lot of people with high potential, top managers, great performers, CEOs, fantastic entrepreneurs, and talented superachievers who have let half their time, energy, and potential slip away because they are in the wrong relationships. They could have accomplished double what they have achieved, and widened their smiles, if they had not drained their power sources. The wrong personal partner is a constant ball and chain.

Therefore, do *not* underestimate the importance of your decision when it comes to settling down with a partner. Just because you are lonely, the hormones are coming out of your ears, or that person just *so* perfectly fits the textbook description of the ideal partner that you have in your mind doesn't make settling for second best any better.

Don't get me wrong: I'm the most stable guy on the planet, and I love to settle down, but I don't like to *settle*! And neither should you.

Check the visions. Sit down; ask relaxed questions. Maybe even get your partner to make a game out of it. It's hard to look the truth in the eye, but just remember this: if *this* is not your ideal partner, then there is someone else out there waiting for you *right now*! And you're wasting your time being with the wrong special someone.

As we've seen, there are plenty of ideal fish in the sea. It's good that you want to commit, but commit to someone from that pool of ideal choices. *Don't settle for less.*

The final step is to compare your visions. Do it. I know, it's hard. Lose the goggles for a second and give your life a lift. The future *you* who is sitting right there on the exotic island with his or her ideal partner will thank you for this.

People who have good relationships at home
are more effective in the marketplace.
—Zig Ziglar

Points to Remember

The question, "Are the visions aligned?" is the most important one in both personal and business relationships.

Whenever you enter into a partnership where the partners' visions and intentions are not aligned, you immediately set yourself up for failure, a lot of friction, stress, and poor or at best mediocre results. This is true for both personal and professional partnerships.

The right people can find you only when you tune in to the desire to find the ideal partner and believe that he or she exists. You can find the ideal partner only if you don't settle. If you settle, this person might be just around the corner, but you're blocking this opportunity because you are still locked into existing relationships, mentally and physically. This applies to any relationships or partnerships, personal or business.

If the person you are with is not your ideal partner in a personal or business relationship, then there is someone else out there waiting for you *right now*, and you're wasting your time and energy with the wrong choice.

Hire or Fire? The Polarity Principle of Relationships, or How to Find the Best People to Work With

Time spent on hiring is time well spent.
—Robert Half

The best and safest thing is to keep a balance in your life,
acknowledge the great powers around us and in us. If you can
do that, and live that way, you are really a wise man.
—Euripides

I asked Richard Branson, founder of the Virgin Group, how he chooses the best people to run his businesses. Richard e-mailed me back saying that he looks for people who really care about others: the ones who are excellent at motivating teams and employees and who always look for the best in people. This last comment especially struck a chord with me. It clearly shows me that Richard always tries to concentrate on the half-full part of the glass, the strengths, unique talents, and gifts that each person brings to the company, not their weaknesses or where they come up short. My take is that this allows him to grow their talents even further up to a point where their unique strong points shine.

Richard went on to say that if the person at the top of a company fits that profile—and is a load of fun at the same time—that person can really take the company to the next level. And if not, they might just as easily destroy it.

Wise words of advice.

Lee Iacocca, former president and CEO of Chrysler, who has been called one of the greatest managers of the last century, once said that the main element in his decision on whether or not to hire somebody was the applicant's sense of humor. Lee said: "After all, I've got to work with this person every day, so it better be fun!" Richard and Lee know that fun produces the best results.

The Polarity Principle: You've Got to Feel Good

You have to be yourself to deliver the best results. And you have to have the feeling that you can be 100 percent yourself with the people around you.

This is what I call the *polarity principle*: whenever you find that you cannot be 100 percent yourself around someone that you're working with on a regular basis, then that person shouldn't be part of your inner core team.

This applies to whatever project, job, business, product, or idea you want to bring to life. It doesn't matter what organization you're in or what your role is: student, trainee, or CEO.

If you don't follow this principle, sooner or later it will lead to a lot of friction that will hurt you, your team, the organization you're working in, and everybody else involved (including your friends, your spouse, or your partner). It will have a devastating impact on performance. And if this is about the person at the top, as Richard said earlier, it can really drive a company into the ground.

You can suppress and impede your energy and identity only so much to try to make relationships work that—in reality—*don't.*

Doing so never pays off.

But She's from MTV!

I once hired a former senior MTV executive for one of my projects who came highly recommended by one of the best concert producers on the planet. Both she and the person recommending her had such an amazing résumé that it was hard not to trust either of them.

Once she started the job, however, my gut was telling me otherwise. I still remember one morning. It was 6 a.m., and I was sitting in my hotel room in Silicon Valley, getting ready for my speech at Google. I had just looked at the first material she had delivered, and it wasn't good. Then I called the expert who had recommended her, and let him talk me into keeping her on the job, although my inner voice still said she wasn't right.

Then, after ploughing through another two hundred e-mails, another ten or twenty phone calls, and some more meetings in Silicon Valley, I forgot all about that inner voice. I simply pushed it aside.

In hindsight, all I needed to do was to believe that new doors would open once I closed old ones. New and great opportunities can appear only after we close the old doors.

Because I was overworked and out of balance, I was happy about having any additional helping hand at all. The result was that she didn't perform and she put the success of the whole organization at risk. In the end, I had to let her go anyway, but I lost many opportunities and could have saved valuable time and money.

Balance Is Key

When you're overworked and out of balance, *any* helping hand will do. This is why balance is key when you're selecting the right people to work with.

I've seen this again and again in my personal experience, especially with personal assistants and general managers. I once got a GM on board for one of my organizations whom I'd never met because I was too busy. I was in such a rush to get somebody started that I made the fatal mistake of not meeting her in person. She came highly recommended, and she had a great CV. It felt good talking to her on the phone, and she seemed to have all the right credentials, so why not?

After months of friction, I let her go. The whole process had a very negative impact on the organization.

Fire Before You Hire

It's a common misconception and standard excuse that you can't fire somebody because you don't have anybody to replace him or her yet. This is not how it works.

You have to fire before you hire.

Go with your gut instincts if you feel that someone isn't working out. Firing someone who isn't the right fit creates a vacuum that will draw the ideal person for that role into your life, project, organization, or business. This works whether you have an organization with thousands of people or whether you're a small group of two, three, or five. It works whether you're a CEO or a housewife selling Tupperware out of her own home with her best friend, who just isn't her best business partner.

It takes courage to go up against what everybody else keeps telling you, especially when you're faced with the opinion of experts in a field where you are an amateur. However, you can be the amateur who just knows better, and that's why you have your gut feeling in the first place.

If you're balanced, your body, your senses, and your intuitions will be telling you something. These are the signals you should listen to. How does it feel to be around this person? Are you excited about getting up in the morning? Are you looking forward to another day of working with this person? Or are you thinking, "Oh my god, not him/her again"?

Be honest with yourself and remember that there is an ideal match for you in whatever organization or life situation you find yourself in.

Our fear that there might not be someone who can fill the position too often encourages us to stay with the wrong choices for far too long. Then our rational mind comes up with all kinds of reasons why we should keep this person—because of her great CV, because he comes highly recommended, because we were told that this was the best person for the job.

If you know, then you know. Act on it or pay dearly later. This goes for all relationships, no matter whether you're dealing with employees, colleagues, coworkers, or even teammates.

If you are in a position to hire or fire, fire! If not, ask to be transferred to another position or to be assigned someone else to work with.

Magic

Why should you leave your gut feelings, intuitive abilities, and everything your senses are telling you out of the equation when you're doing business? The answer is simple: you shouldn't.

Musicians can create masterpieces if they are playing with the right people. Great friends can create unforgettable moments. Great athletes can forever surpass themselves once they are teamed up with the right players.

In the same way, the right team—even if it's a team of two—can create magic. Never underestimate this element of magic in producing spectacular results that can leave the world, and yourself, in awe. You cannot plan for it, but you can create the right circumstances to make magic come to life by choosing the right people to work with.

Director James Cameron put it well: "The magic doesn't come from within the director's mind, it comes from within the hearts of the actors."

EXERCISE: Find the Black Sheep
Time needed: 7 minutes

Make a list of everybody you are working with on a regular basis. If you want to spend more time, make a similar list of friends and family members. You might even put your life partner or spouse on that list.

Then be honest with yourself and apply the polarity principle. Hire or fire. If you could honestly separate yourself from any or all of these individuals, which ones would you cross out?

It takes guts to do that. I've seen people cross out their life partner or spouse, but in the end they were truly relieved, and everything was for the better.

With billions of people living on this planet today, there is truly the perfect match for everything and everyone in every area of your life. Remind yourself of this fact and it will give you the courage to make the difficult and uncomfortable decisions when you have to.

There is no "i" in team, but there is in win.
—Michael Jordan

As brilliant an individual that Michael Jordan was,
he was not successful until he got with a good team unit.
—Kareem Abdul-Jabbar

Points to Remember

Whenever you find that you cannot be 100 percent yourself around someone that you're working with on a regular basis, then that person shouldn't be part of your inner core team.

If you are in a position to hire or fire, fire! If not, ask to be transferred to another position or to be assigned someone else to work with.

When you're overworked and out of balance, *any* helping hand will do. This is why balance is key when you're selecting the right people to work with. You have to fire before you hire. New and great opportunities can appear only after we close the old doors.

Go with your gut instincts if you feel someone isn't working out. Firing someone who isn't the right fit creates a vacuum that will draw the ideal person for that role into your life, project, or business.

Believe that new doors will open once you close the old ones. New and great opportunities can appear only after we close the old doors.

The right team—even if it's a team of two—can create magic. Never underestimate this element of magic in producing spectacular results that can leave the world, and yourself, in awe.

Suggested Reading:
The Few Books That Really Matter

I love to read. But I agree with author Timothy Ferriss that in today's world, a low-information diet is the only way to go. That said, here are a few books that really matter. You don't need to read any of them in order to do what this book promises, but if you want to dig down in a particular area, go for it!

Some of them have changed my life.

For additional book recommendations and resource material, visit our comprehensive companion site: www.nothingisimpossible.co.

Managing Oneself, by Peter Drucker. You have to know how to manage yourself. This is true whether you are an artist, a student, just starting out on the corporate ladder, or a housewife with four kids. When it comes to getting to know yourself, Peter Drucker is the best in the field. Are you a reader or a listener? How do you process information? If you're stuck in a particular area, it's probably because you don't know yourself well enough. This book was an eye-opener for me.

Walden, by Henry David Thoreau. This takes me back to my days at Choate Rosemary Hall, my U.S. boarding school. It is a masterpiece when it comes to finding yourself and following your true calling. You won't be disappointed!

Force of Nature, by Laird Hamilton. I talk a lot about being in sync with your body and using it as one of your prime decision-making tools. If you still don't know what somebody who rides 35-foot waves at 60 mph can teach you about realizing your full potential, think again. This is highly recommended for all the CEOs and entrepreneurs out there who regularly forget about putting their bodies first.

Secrets of Power Negotiating: Inside Secrets from a Master Negotiator, by Roger Dawson. Have you ever wondered why some deals fall through and others are accomplished with ease? Then this book is for you. It's an eye-opener and the best practical tool there is when it comes to negotiating. If you read this, you are in for a ride. From now on, prepare yourself to turn every no into a yes.

The Science of Persuasion, by Robert Cialdini. Cialdini is the real deal, and I mean it. If you want to know how to convince anybody of anything, to prepare the best elevator pitch in the world, and to become a genius at social dynamics in business and in life, then this book is highly recommended. I make it a must-read for all my global MBA students.

Predictably Irrational, by Dan Ariely. Ariely and Cialdini are indispensable on your road to success if you want to become a master of persuasion and influence. Ariely will teach you how to structure any offer for your service or product, even if it's yourself you are offering in that next job interview.

The Four-Hour Workweek, by Timothy Ferriss. Tim has spawned a whole series of books, from *The Four-Hour Workweek* to *The Four-Hour Body* to *The Four-Hour Chef*. His approach is simple: what are the tiniest steps you can take that will produce the biggest results?

The Tao of Physics, by Fritjof Capra. When I went to business school and was still planning to go to Wall Street afterward, I read an article about a guy who had made $250 million in investment banking. The only two books he recommended were *The Tao of Physics* and *The Dancing Wu Li Masters*. It took me two years of intensive study to figure out why these were so instrumental to his success. I was obsessed with it until I cracked the stock market code. Then the gates of Midas opened up! I will say no more. You have to figure this one out for yourself.

Like a Virgin, by Richard Branson. Richard recommended this book to me before it came out, and it is his latest one. All of Richard's books are pearls of wisdom. There's no nonsense, just real-life wisdom from a man who has done it all and will serve as an inspiration for generations to come. Global business renegade, passionate kitesurfer, and a true believer in world peace—what more can you want from a guy?

Secrets of the Millionaire Mind, by Harv T. Eker. This one is an eye-opener when it comes to wealth creation and freeing yourself from limiting beliefs that keep you from abundance.

The Millionaire Mind Course, by Marc Allen. Marc is a good friend and a true inspiration of ease and effortlessness in action. This title is one of his best. It's one of the top 10 books I recommend to friends.

The Artist's Way, by Julia Cameron. When it comes to creativity, letting yourself go, and watching the magic happen, Julia presents a perfect plan for discovering the artist within. While this book is written for artists, you will know by now that I think we are all creative geniuses. This book will help you uncover the sides and talents you did not know you had.

The Seth Material, by Jane Roberts. The Seth material covers a wide range of different topics and laid the foundation for the New Age era. I honestly believe that hundreds of other books that followed are just variations on Seth's basic themes, including the law of attraction.

Enough to Go Around: Searching for Hope in Afghanistan, Pakistan and Darfur, by Chip Duncan. Imagine your village destroyed and your family murdered in genocide. Writer/photographer Chip Duncan takes readers on a journey through three of the world's most challenging places. What he finds—hope—might surprise you.

Search Inside Yourself, by Chade-Meng Tan. I was one of the first Meng asked to have a look at the drafts of his book, and I still feel honored. I saw it evolve from concept to finished product to worldwide success. Meng is not only one of my best friends, but also a firm supporter of and believer in world peace. This book is a groundbreaking example of how one single individual can change the culture of a corporate giant such as Google and inspire thousands of others to do the same. Meng is the real deal, and I recommend this highly. In this book, I talk about how important it is to achieve inner peace, and Meng's bible is a fantastic guide loaded with tons of practical exercises.

The Alchemist, by Paulo Coelho. This book is one of the bestselling books of all time. It has left a deep impression not only on me, but on countless others, including Hollywood actor Will Smith, presidents, Nobel laureates, and CEOs. Why? Its appeal is universal, and its style is simple. Paulo speaks right to your heart in a modern-day fable that encourages you to go for your dreams, no matter what. Then, as Paulo says, the whole universe will conspire to make them reality.

The Seven Spiritual Laws of Success and *Peace Is the Way*, by Deepak Chopra. These are just two titles out of an enormous collection by an extraordinary writer, speaker, visionary, and good friend.

Audio Books

Stephen King was the first to get me hooked on the idea that you can read much more when you listen to audio books while you are doing something else (working out, shopping, and so on).

I am a verbal processor (which means that I learn best by hearing myself talk). This also means that I am a listener (which means that I absorb, learn, and process information best if it is in audio form). If you're the same, then audio books are definitely the way to go.

In no particular order, here are a few to get you started.

Business Stripped Bare and *Losing My Virginity*, by Richard Branson. There's no need to introduce the man any further. These books are the real deal. What I like most about Richard is that he actually reads his books himself, unlike some other hotshots, who are way too busy to record their own audio books. This just goes to show that Richard really cares about his readers.

Get the Life You Want, by Richard Bandler. Bandler was one of the fathers of neuro-linguistic programming (NLP), which became the basis of many bestsellers, including the ones by self-help author Anthony Robbins. This book presents the foundation of NLP and is one of the best introductions to the subject.

Wherever You Go, There You Are, by John Kabat-Zinn. This is a classic in the area of mindfulness and meditation. It goes hand in hand with the concept described in this book, that the more you are one with what you are doing, the more you will use all of your senses, the more you will have all your powers and skills available, and the more you can push the boundaries of what you thought was possible. If you want a booster to get you into the zone even faster, read John's book.

Bonus Material

For much more reader-only content, free bonus material, and success stories, visit our comprehensive companion site: www.nothingisimpossible.co.

Do you want to join the new class of high achievers? Join us and see how simple it is.

Check out my personal website for my speeches, my music, my foundation and philanthropy, and my daily adventures around the globe, from kitesurfing big waves in Cape Town to helping underprivileged kids in Mumbai: www.tom-oliver.com.

If you would like to get in touch with me personally to share your own success stories, ask for advice, or to take yourself, your idea, product, brand, or business to the next level, please feel free to contact me at:

nothingisimpossible@tom-oliver.com.

Acknowledgments

This is a little bit like giving an Oscar acceptance speech. You don't want to forget anyone! I want to thank and acknowledge the many fantastic people who have made this book possible:

First and foremost, my parents. Thanks to my dad for being there all the way, from my days at Choate to Wharton to my music to the World Peace Foundation to the many ventures we have been in together. Your loyalty is outstanding. You are not only the best dad I could ever wish for, but also my best friend and advisor, and you always will be.

To my mother for showing me the true value of speech and that a word can change worlds.

Thanks to my wife for showing me the Brazilian way to a happy life, the *sempre da un geito* (there is always a way), for gently guiding me along the way, and for reminding the utter perfectionist in me again and again of the fact that doing 51 percent is better than not getting anything done at all.

To the Dalai Lama for showing me the Golden Rule and how to deal with energy, besides inspiring love and kindness. I will never forget our first private meeting, with the Secret Service at the front door and the bomb squad surrounding the building. You will shine as an inspiration for generations to come.

To Desmond Tutu for teaching me *Ubuntu* and believing in the power of the impossible and that we all can make a difference. Thanks for all your support, from the very first private service in the Anglican cathedral in Cape Town to your support for our launch in Berlin.

To Richard Branson for showing us all again and again that business and fun are brothers and not mutually exclusive. You are a living example that nothing is impossible! We have so much in common, from our passion for kitesurfing to our dedication to the nonconformist life-style to our belief in world peace—you as a founder of the Elders, me as a founder of the World Peace Foundation. Thanks for all your continued help, feedback, and support in making dreams come true.

To Jeff Skoll for constantly inspiring the social entrepreneur in all of us. You shine a light not only through the Skoll Foundation but also through your unwavering personal commitment and dedication to making this world a better place. And, last but not least, for "making movies that make change" through Participant Media—the kind of movies that inspire and motivate us to create a better reality where truly nothing is impossible.

To Jez Frampton of Interbrand for believing in the timeless principles in this book and their immense value for corporate success. No wonder you're the number one authority on branding in the world! Your line "businesses don't jam enough" has become my favorite. Looking forward to many more adventures together—and lots more jamming!

Thanks to my English teacher at Choate Rosemary Hall, Chuck D. Timlin, for believing in the author in me and nurturing my love for writing and speaking at the time when it mattered most. That's when the author was born who wrote this book.

Thanks to my agent, Bill Gladstone of Waterside, for demystifying the publishing process and creating a "stripping away of the inessential," as J. K. Rowling would say. It was love at first sight—a truly ideal partnership! Thanks for your guidance.

To the whole team at McGraw-Hill for feeling the same enthusiasm and passion about this project as I do. Especially to my editor, Tom Miller, who shares my passion for languages. You rock! And of course to Mary Glenn, my publisher. You even share my love of the ocean and shell rings. It made the cover!

To Ervin Laszlo, founder of the Club Budapest, for showing me that a mind can be at the peak of its brilliance at the age of 80. Your work remains a constant inspiration.

To the Dalai Lama and Tenzin Tethong, founder of the Dalai Lama Foundation, for inviting me to join the Committee of 100 for Tibet, and for still believing in peace when others have given up hope. I will always be at your side.

To Paulo Coelho for showing me that the "book is the boss" and for our enlightening conversations in Portuguese.

To Peggy Dulany, who has created something that few others could dream of: the best circle of global philanthropists on the planet. Each member of the Global Philanthropists Circle is a reflection of who you are: a kind, loving, and caring individual who always places others first and constantly believes in the greater good of this planet and humanity. You are a beacon of light who reminds us of the one thing that is truly worth fighting and living for: a better tomorrow.

To Mickey Eskimo for showing me what it takes to kitesurf a 30-foot wave. You are truly something!

To Russell James for believing in world peace and being such a good friend. You have a heart of gold.

Thanks to will.i.am for inspiring me to write a chapter about success principles. You are not only a talented singer and songwriter, but also a gifted entrepreneur and philanthropist.

Thanks to my good friend and brother Chade-Meng Tan for sharing and supporting my dream and passion for world peace, for being a constant source of inspiration, and for bringing some of my best "aha" moments to life. You showed me the value of happiness as our default state of mind. You will always be in my heart.

To Chip Duncan, my good friend and fellow warrior of light, for all your continued support, help, advice, and strength. You're not only one of the most outstanding filmmakers, photographers, and writers, but a caring individual who always thinks about the world at large and who believes in the good in all of us. Thanks for being such a loyal friend and supporter of world peace over the years. Glad to be with you on this journey.

To Hugh Evans, cofounder and CEO of the Global Poverty Project and founder of Make Poverty History. Your unwavering dedication to making this world a better place is a true inspiration. I've said it many times, and I will say it again: you are one of the most intelligent and outstanding individuals I've ever met.

To all the global advisors and supporters of the World Peace Foundation and the World Peace Festival. You have made my journey the path of a warrior of light.

Thanks to the whole team at Interbrand over the years, from Gion-Men Kruegel-Hanna to Harald Moench, for turning my visions into hard facts. You are masters at branding.

To the team at Saatchi & Saatchi, especially Richard Huntington, for being so brilliant at creating blueprints for global movements out of a vision and a passion.

To all the eight thousand kids and students from around the world at the World Peace Congress in Mumbai. You remind me daily why inspiration, vision, and passion are so important. I applaud your hearts, your dreams, and your gratitude. You are our future.

To all the kids in Dharavi and the other slums around the world for your smiles and your gratitude that lights up my world and reminds me of what truly matters: that altruism is the biggest egoism. Or, as Desmond Tutu would say, "I am because you are."

To Dr. Varadarajan at NES for opening the gates to India's most talented and brightest next-generation leaders.

To author Tess Gerrittsen for showing me what it takes to become a dedicated author and writer.

To Deepak Chopra for sharing our common dream of world peace and for being an inspiration and a beacon of light. Thanks for all your continued support. I always admire how you keep so many balls in the air! We definitely have to do projects in India together.

To Bono for showing me that being a rock star, having fun, and changing the world can be one and the same thing. You inspire greatness in all of us, from student to CEO.

To Internet entrepreneur, author, and philanthropist Bill Liao for sharing my dream of world peace, believing in me from the start, and always being there for the cause. The world needs more people like you.

Thanks to Sharon Stone for showing me the true value of education and what it means to stand up for yourself from the moment we first met at the Beverly Hills Hotel. You taught me to believe in my personal story. You are not only eternal charisma in action, but also one of the most intelligent people I know.

To Peter Buffett, gifted musician and one of the leading philanthropists in the world, for showing us how to have a big vision and a big heart and how to constantly reinvent ourselves.

To Brigitte and Liz Mohn of Bertelsmann for being inspiring philanthropists, for regularly bringing the best global leaders together to address the most pressing challenges humanity faces today—and for giving me a special role in this worthwhile endeavor.

Thanks to Denise Hayward, my loyal personal assistant, for her many years of constant dedication, calm, and patience and for being the backbone of my organization.

Thanks to Christian Obad for sharing a great ride for so many years. It wasn't meant to be a business partnership for life, but we have become great friends in the process! Your loyalty is outstanding. Thanks for being there in the good and the challenging times.

Thanks to Rick Stack, advisor, teacher, author, entrepreneur, and friend, for taking me down the rabbit hole as far as I wanted to go and for all your loyal support over the years. You are amazing!

Thanks to "Jamaica Dave" Brooks for opening countless doors to make the network even bigger and your unwavering commitment to making this world a better place.

Thanks to Michael Luger, dean of Manchester Business School, for approaching me after my keynote address at the European Parliament and inviting me to come to Manchester for my lecture. It was the birth of the Leadership Circle.

Thanks to all my global MBA students, from Manchester to Kellogg, and especially the students in my Leadership Circle at Manchester Business School. You provided valuable feedback and success stories. And most of all, thanks for asking your most pressing questions. You all helped me to cut to the chase and concentrate on what really produces results. You have inspired me to refine the principles even more and look at your challenges, questions, and needs from a new perspective.

A special thanks goes to Uzayr Ali, who was so instrumental in bringing the Leadership Circle to life. Thanks to Elaine Ferneley, director of the MBA program at Manchester Business School, for her continued support. Hope you're still doing the Hour of Power!

Thanks to Felix Petry, my loyal band leader, for our countless jamming and live sessions that indirectly have contributed so much to this book.

Thanks to all the loyal members of my team and staff over the years who have helped me make the impossible reality. There are far more of you than I could ever list in this book. Special gratitude and thanks to Hanna Nyholm, Chris Blackburn, Wolfram Lutz, Mike Anson, and all the countless others around the world. None of this would have been possible without you.

Last but not least, to all you high achievers out there who have urged me to write this book. You constantly show us that nothing is impossible! This book is for you, by you, and because of you. May your light shine and convince us all that we are capable of so much more.

Index

About the Author

Tom Oliver is a businessman, global social entrepreneur, artist, philanthropist, and visionary who has worked with some of the world's leading figures, such as Desmond Tutu, the Dalai Lama, and the CEOs of several Fortune 500 companies.

Tom Oliver is the founder and Chair of the global Leadership Circle at the Manchester Business School in the United Kingdom, where he teaches and mentors MBA students from dozens of countries. Oliver grew up in Germany and the United States; he attended the Wharton School of Finance and Commerce at the University of Pennsylvania and completed a master's degree in economics at the University of Cologne in Germany.

Oliver is the founder and CEO of the World Peace Foundation and the founder of the World Peace Festival, which Nobel Peace Prize laureate Desmond Tutu called "the most influential peace gathering in history." The World Peace Foundation has been supported by many dignitaries and Nobel Prize laureates and by an impressive list of international partners, including the United Nations, Virgin, and Google, philanthropists such as Peter Buffett, and business leaders such as Richard Branson.

Oliver's expertise is sought after by corporations including Google, financial institutions such as the World Bank, and business schools such as Kellogg School of Management. The European Parliament, the UN, and several governments including those of Austria and China have invited Tom to address the world's leaders.

Tom Oliver is dedicated to the concept of business as a catalyst for social change. He has been a member of the Global Philanthropists Circle, which includes 70 of the leading philanthropic families in the world. Oliver´s work has received numerous awards and recognitions, among them the title of "Best practices and innovations in individual philanthropy and social investment around the world" by the Synergos Institute. Oliver has been awarded a lifelong seat as a creative member in the think tank the Club of Budapest and a lifelong seat as a distinguished member in the Committee of the 100 for Tibet.

Tom Oliver is also a renowned singer and songwriter, artist, pianist, and music producer. As a live performer, he has headlined festivals around the world.

Oliver is also a passionate surfer, kitesurfer, and kung fu black belt.

He speaks five languages fluently (German, English, French, Italian, and Portuguese) and divides his time between the South of France, Germany, and New York.

For more information, see www.tom-oliver.com